Chas Newkey-Burden is the author of a number of books including *The Reduced History Of Britain* and *The All-New Official Arsenal Miscellany*. He also contributed to both *Crap Towns* books. His work regularly appears in a range of magazines and newspapers.

GREAT EMAIL DISASTERS

CHAS NEWKEY-BURDEN

JOHN BLAKE

Published by Metro Publishing Ltd,
3 Bramber Court, 2 Bramber Road,
London W14 9PB, England

www.blake.co.uk

First published in paperback in 2007

ISBN: 978-1-84454-410-3

British Library Cataloguing-in-Publication Data:

A catalogue record for this book is available from the British Library.

Design by www.envydesign.co.uk

Printed in the UK by CPI Bookmarque, Croydon, CR0 4TD

1 3 5 7 9 10 8 6 4 2

Papers used by Metro Publishing are natural, recyclable
products made from wood grown in sustainable forests.
The manufacturing processes conform to the environmental
regulations of the country of origin.

This book is dedicated to Chris

ACKNOWLEDGEMENTS

Thanks to Rosie Ries, Michelle Signore and Lucian Randall of John Blake Publishing who came up with the idea for this book and to Mike Mosedale for his excellent cartoon. Particular gratitude is due to Lucian for his support, wit, alcohol and expertise throughout the process. Thanks to John Blake for giving me the deal and making me part of such a fantastic publishing operation.

I also wish to thank: Sam Jordison, Bill Borrows, Matt Ford, Judy Kerr, Eleanor Levy, Martin Corteel, Roland Hall, Trevor Davies, Sam Pilger, Joe Parry, Yaara Shalom, Will Jessop, Alex Hannaford, Susi Weizmann and, of course, Bibi.

Special thanks and love to Chris Morris and Julie Burchill for their encouragement, love, wisdom and unflinching ability to help me think big.

CONTENTS

INTRODUCTION

The chances are you've bought this book to have a good laugh at other people's misfortunes. If so, welcome – you've come to the right place! There is enough here to satisfy the most gluttonous gloater. Crammed full of tales of people who have fallen prey to email humiliation, this book spares no blushes.

However, while you are cackling away at misfortunes of others, keep in mind that, statistically speaking, there is a good chance that you too will soon become the victim of a great email disaster. A survey by the search engine Lycos has claimed that 42 email mistakes are made every minute in the United Kingdom. According to the same survey, 60 per cent of us have sent an email to the wrong person and 33 per cent of these messages included steamy images or text. The survey also found that nearly a quarter of wrongly addressed emails were mocking the very person they were accidentally sent to.

Meanwhile, a different survey carried out among businesses across the UK in 2006 found that the workplace is fertile ground for keyboard catastrophes. A third of UK companies polled had fired staff for violating email policies during the previous 12 months and over 70 per cent had disciplined staff for the same reason. A similar survey in America found that 21 per cent of employers had been involved in court cases in which their staff's email had been called as evidence.

The great email disaster has entered public consciousness to such an extent that it has also cropped up in fictional drama. In the first series of the smash-hit television series *The Office*,

Wernham Hogg regional manager David Brent is showing Donna, a work-experience girl and daughter of a friend, around the company's office in Slough. He pauses at a colleague's computer to show Donna how email works and is confronted with an email that portrays him, as he puts it, 'as a woman with two men doing *that* all over me'. When he asks his staff how many of them have seen the email, all put their hands up, including Joan the cleaner who doesn't even have access to email. 'Someone printed it off for me,' she explains.

Email disasters can strike anyone. The stories in this book involve everyone from an unknown romantic poet in Slough to a Westminster spin doctor, a television celebrity and a leading US politician. Nobody who switches on a computer is safe.

Ever since they were invented, computers have had the capacity to terrify the human race. From the start, people have worried that high technology will make them redundant at work. Parents fear that their children might fall victim to paedophiles in internet chat rooms. Others are concerned that online chat will destroy youngsters' ability to speak correct English and end face-to-face conversation.

Some scientists warn that, ultimately, computers will take over the world. There is no sign of a computer master race just yet, but perhaps the biggest threat that computers pose to us is through email. In the olden days, it was unlikely that you would walk to your local post office and accidentally send a letter with sensitive details of your love-life to 10 million complete strangers. Thanks to email – and with the help of mischievous people across the planet who are always happy to forward embarrassing messages to their friends – you can do just that in an instant.

The lack of caution shown by many of the protagonists in these stories is surprising. None of our victims has followed the basic rule of email, which is to never put into an email anything that you would not be happy to say out loud, in front of your grandmother or in court.

If only Cherie Blair had thought of that before she chatted online with Peter Foster about how he was helping her buy property. How Claire Swires must have wished she had followed it before she discussed fellatio with her lover. Why didn't Trevor Luxton think of it before emailing his mates to brag about how he had cheated on his girlfriend while he was on the phone to her? And how many people would still have their jobs if they had just thought before they sent that fateful email?

Fortunately for us, the world is full of people lacking in caution. Beginning with tales of humiliation from the pre-email era – involving fax fuck-ups, terrible telegrams and loquacious love letters – this book will show how cyberspace has become a fertile ground for utter humiliation.

And such entertaining humiliation! A politician is hounded out of office, a headmaster is humiliated, a teenager is electronically tagged by a court and a woman receives an email reporting her own death. All along the way, relationships are left in tatters and Robert Kilroy-Silk is left standing in a car park, covered in actual poo. Email: we salute you!

I hope you'll enjoy these stories, but, when you've finished laughing at the poor unfortunates in them, make a mental note to take care when you next open your email program. An 'email etiquette' guide is included at the end of the book to help you reduce the chances of your own humiliation. After all, the penalties for cocking up over email are huge and I'd hate you to become the victim of a great email disaster yourself. Though please let me know if you do – I'd love to write a sequel!

Just when you thought it was safe to switch on your computer – along comes *Great Email Disasters*!

CHAPTER ONE

FAX ME! – PRE-EMAIL DISASTERS

It seems almost shocking to recall that, not so long ago, email did not exist. Trust me, I've fact-checked this thoroughly and it is definitely true.

Apparently, even now there are some people who do not use email. For most of us, though, it is now such a familiar part of our everyday existence that we simply take it for granted. It is hard to imagine that there was a time when 'Yahoo!' was simply something you shouted when you got overexcited; when 'hotmail' was something women said if they saw an attractive man; when an attachment was what a married couple felt for one another; and when 'Lol' was an abbreviation of Lawrence.

We have become such cyber junkies that it is hard to imagine life before email. Just what did people *do* all day? Work, I suppose.

However, all that was to change in October 1971 when Ray Tomlinson – who worked for US-based computer company Bolt, Beranek and Newman – developed a way for computers across the globe to communicate with one another. He also chose the '@' symbol to break up email addresses, the first of which was his: tomlinson@bbn-tenexa. (The .com and related suffixes came along later.) Tomlinson cannot remember the text of his first email message, but suspects it was something like 'qwertyuiop' or 'testing 1-2-3'.

How disappointing. This hardly ranks alongside the first words ever sent via telegram 'What hell hath God wrought?' – or the first words spoken over the telephone – 'Mr Watson, come here. I want you.' However, people whose disastrous email mistakes are recounted in the coming pages would probably give their right arm to swap the content of their fatal messages with such a banal text as Tomlinson's.

Although the medium's roots lie in the 1970s, email did not come into widespread use until the 1990s when we all began to sign up, log on and send off. With a wicked glint in its eye, evolution had given us a form of communication that was ripe for comedy, disaster and humiliation. Not that communication was a safe place in pre-email days. Throughout history, the human race has found ways to mess up and shower itself in ignominy while communicating with its fellow men and women.

In 1779, for example, when the young Prince of Wales went to watch a performance of *A Winter's Tale*, he was rather taken by Mary Robinson, the young lady playing the part of Perdita, the heroine of the play. The young prince – later to become King George IV – sent an underling to seek out her feelings about the two of them embarking on a mouth-open-with-tongues type of relationship. If this seems a rather impersonal way to go about winning her heart, then the Prince of Wales soon made up for it with some thoroughly passionate and steamy love letters.

These letters came back to haunt him when their affair ended a year later. There was already intense speculation in the press about their relationship. The *Morning Post* and *Morning Herald* were publishing gossipy articles and cartoons about the pair. So, when the Prince of Wales dumped her, Robinson had her revenge by demanding £25,000 for the return of his steamy love letters. In the end she settled for a £5,000 pay-off to return the letters after King George III decided he had no option but to pay up 'to get my son out of this shameful scrape'.

Those who do not study history, it has been said, are doomed to repeat it. Just prior to the 1997 general election, another public figure got himself into a scrape by sending some love letters. A male researcher claimed that he had been enjoying an affair with married Conservative MP Jerry Hayes. Hayes admitted the pair enjoyed a close friendship but denied that the pair had ever bought tickets to the coital arena.

This denial would have carried more weight

had the researcher not been able to call on a series of letters that Hayes had sent him. 'I love you,' one began. 'I really am trying very hard to forget you but I just can't. I miss your daft voice, your smile, your laughter melting into your eyes. I feel a bit like the guy in the old movies who will do anything for the one he loves and ends up charging down the aisle on a white charger and full armour! I know that's silly but so am I.'

You said it, Jerry!

Another reads: 'I've just been crying my eyes out. I just can't help it. I love you with every fibre of my being. Honestly, I wish I didn't but I can't help myself.

'When I saw you looking so beautiful, so radiant, so loving on Friday night I really thought you wanted to make a go of it again. I am stupid enough to say that I would give anything up for you ... that I would love you until my dying day.' This paper trail certainly played a major part in Hayes losing his seat in the 1997 general election and blighted a once promising political career. Nowadays, he is a barrister.

If you think Hayes's words were cringeworthy,

wait until you read the love letters sent by former Chief of Defence Staff Sir Peter Harding to Lady Bienvenida Buck, the wife of Conservative MP Sir Antony Buck. 'You have maturity beyond your years, yet the body of a young girl. You have experienced so much of life, yet have the beauty of the unscathed,' he dribbled in ink.

'Your face is serene. Your eyes piercing, your mouth enchanting, your back elegant, your hands so graceful, your skin so very fair and satin to touch, your nipples so delicately pink, like a girl, your breasts so petite, your legs so gazelle-like, your smell so overpoweringly intoxicating. How I long to hold you in my arms, to crush you, to envelop you in kisses, to caress you.'

Don't look away just yet, there's more...

'You are all in a woman that I love and hope for; on top of that is you, Bienvenida, the person ... I catch glimpses of a little girl who needs cherishing and loving as we all do and then I long to call you "my little one".'

And more...

'I adore you, Bienvenida; I love you more than I can express. As I looked into your beautiful eyes last evening and you wept a little, I was moved beyond measure. We must develop together and then take on the world. Growing together, loving together, getting ever closer, building a new world for us. We both know the constraints but we will work even harder to overcome them, I know. Life is empty when you are not there.'

Life became even emptier for Sir Peter when Buck sold these letters for £175,000 and Sir Peter was forced to resign from his post. Funny that anyone would pay £175,000 to read Sir Peter blabbering on about elegant backs and girl-like pink nipples. I think a lot of people would pay to *avoid* having to read about it.

It isn't just letters that have seen the powerful come a cropper. Faxes, too, have the potential for disaster and embarrassment. Former Tory MP Jonathan Aitken had a highly embarrassing time when a sensitive fax about the arms-to-Iran scandal was accidentally sent to a journalist. Indeed, faxes are so often sent to the wrong person that many of them now routinely include a disclaimer at the bottom of the message, telling anybody who might receive it by accident to destroy it and disregard the contents.

No chance of that when the accidental recipient is a gossipy old journalist. In 2004, top-secret plans for Tony Blair's holiday in Tuscany were drawn up to be faxed to police stations in the region. However, the sender accidentally faxed them direct to 15 Tuscan news organisations. 'This has really put the cat among the pigeons,' said a source from the Blair camp. 'Things may well have to be altered now because we don't know where this fax ended up.' (As we will see later on, email would be even more disastrous to Blair's administration.)

Then there is a story of a detective who sent the same fax to a colleague over and over again one afternoon. When the colleague phoned him and asked him to stop, the detective replied that he thought the fax hadn't gone through, because it kept coming out of the other end of his own fax machine.

This story cannot be verified, so it is perhaps apocryphal, but it is perfectly plausible given other fax errors the boys in blue have committed. After all, when Maxine Carr, the ex-girlfriend of Soham murderer Ian Huntley, was released from prison, top-secret details of plans for her future in a safe house and a new identity were accidentally faxed by Humberside police to two young businessmen, who then tried to sell the fax to the highest bidder.

But anything policemen can do, doctors can do better. Landlord Michael Finnerty, who runs a pub in Portsmouth, was stunned when one day his fax machine spat out highly confidential medical details of local people, including accounts of sexual abuse they had suffered. He reported the error to the sender but the faxes kept arriving for up to 12 months. The faxes were intended for a social services office, which had a similar fax number.

The *Evening Standard* had to grovel to Labour MP Bryan Gould after it published an article under his byline which he had not written, a cock-up caused by a mishap at their fax machine. The newspaper's editor Stewart Steven – whose catchphrases included 'When everything is crashing around you, keep smiling' and 'Beware the person in an organisation who has never made a mistake' –

said, 'I and the *Evening Standard* wish whole-heartedly to apologise to Mr Gould. I wish to assure him and the Labour Party that there was no malign intention.

'A series of errors was made and by extra-ordinary mischance the article commissioned from Mr Gould came over on the fax at almost exactly the same time as another article, not commissioned and with no name on it, arrived from someone else.

'There was quite simply confusion in the office, as a result of which Mr Gould's own article was never put into the editorial system. This is, of course, inexcusable and a full-scale inquiry as to exactly how this could have occurred continues.'

The farcical chain of events the inquiry uncovered made for hilarious reading. The published article had been written by none other than Nicholas Howard, the teenage son of Conservative MP Michael Howard. The aspiring journalist had faxed the article to a number of newspapers in the hope they might publish it.

Howard's article began: 'I was three and a half during the winter of discontent.' This should have been a give-away to the editorial team at the *Evening Standard* that something was wrong, as Mr Gould would have been 39 during the winter of discontent. The *Evening Standard* team said that they had assumed that Gould was imagining himself, for the purposes of the column, to be a first-time voter.

The article went on to slag off Tony Blair. How much more evidence did the *Evening Standard* folk need to realise that this article was not penned by Labour diehard Bryan Gould? The 'Bryan Gould fax-up' episode won the Fiasco of the Year gong in the Media Guardian awards for 1995.

In 1987, Germaine Greer accidentally faxed her regular column for *The Times* to the *Independent* newspaper. On learning of her error, she decided to stay with the *Independent* after all. Years later, an email slip-up would prove, as we shall see, utterly disastrous to another newspaper columnist.

But, before we turn to email, let's take a quick look at the medium's closest relation – the telegram. As numerous military leaders of yesteryear would attest, it was a hugely disaster-prone medium. Many had their plans intercepted by the enemy with horrific consequences. Then there was the woman in Prussia who insisted that her local telegram office should telegraph some sauerkraut to her soldier son who was fighting the French. 'He was called up to war by telegram,' she reasoned. 'If you can send my son to war via telegram, then you can send him some food via telegram too.'

Obviously, it is not possible to send food via email either, but email has been responsible for a rich feast of embarrassment. The stories that follow thoroughly out-blush any humiliation that post, phone, fax or telegram have wrought on the human race. Enjoy these great email disasters.

CHAPTER TWO

THE OFFICE

(PART ONE)

I t would normally be easy to feel sorry for a man who lost his job as the result of a great email disaster. However, anyone who quotes catchphrases from breakfast-cereal commercials really deserves everything they get.

She was a grrrrrrrreat shag as well

In 2000, John Crook was a senior personnel manager with Manpower Services plc, where he was said to earn £24,500 per year. When he recommended one of his colleagues, Jeanette Neale, for a small pay rise, Crook's line manager

Angela Brunton emailed him to ask why he felt Neale deserved the rise.

Crook replied, 'She has run both businesses in Norwich during Amee's and Lesley's annual leave and has recruited and retained a 100 per cent training school all on her tod.' So far, so good, but then, he added his punchline: 'She was a grrrrrrrrrreat shag as well.'

Oh dear, oh dear. When Brunton received the email, her PA – who one suspects needs to get out a bit more – saw the email and complained about the comment. Crook was fired for gross misconduct. He immediately appealed and took his former employers to an industrial tribunal, claiming unfair dismissal.

During the tribunal's hearing at Bury St Edmunds, Suffolk in 2001, Crook put up quite a fight. He argued that the email was written as part of a general atmosphere of smuttiness at the firm. 'It was in the context of a culture I'd become accustomed to,' he said. Crook also claimed that Brunton's original email had included some innuendo, reading, 'What has she done to demonstrate her worth and how was it measured?' Crook insisted that their email exchange was 'the kind of dialogue to which I had been accustomed'.

He added, 'Knowing Angela as I did, and yes I knew her as a responsible business manager but also as a fun-loving person, the day I read her email, my perception was that it contained innuendo that was basically invoking innuendo.'

Coming out with all guns blazing, Crook added that he and his line manager were very close friends. 'We knew each other affectionately,' he said. He claimed that he had partied with Brunton at conferences and had been in her hotel room when she straddled a male colleague as he lay bare-chested on the bed. She then shaved her co-worker's chin, claimed Crook. He also said he'd seen her participate in a competition to see who could dance closest to the floor. Crook added that Brunton once kissed him 'amorously' in a bar and that he had once seen Brunton kiss a female manager – with tongues.

Never a dull moment at Manpower! Well, maybe not. Brunton denied both kissing incidents and snapped that what she did away from work was 'her own business'. She said of

Crook's email, 'I didn't take it as a joke at the time. I just thought the tone of the response was totally inappropriate.'

There was never any suggestion that Crook and Neale had engaged in any form of sexual relationship. Indeed, Neale was one of the few people involved who saw the email for what it was. 'It didn't really affect me,' she said. 'There was nothing in what he said in the email. It was just John being his jokeful self. Nothing he said was ever meant in harm or in a sexual nature.' Crook – who went on to set up his own recruitment firm – also received support from his wife who said: 'What's happened to him seems very harsh and unfair.'

However, no amount of support was enough to get Crook his job back. The tribunal chairman John Wheeldon accepted that the email was a joke and admitted that it was possible to construe innuendo in Brunton's original email. However, he rejected Crook's claim of unfair dismissal. 'We consider that a man in Mr Crook's position should have not responded to the innuendo that he thought was there in the way he did.'

Crook remained unrepentant. He called the tribunal verdict a 'farce' and said it 'devastated' him. He raged, 'The joke is that the Austin Powers film *The Spy Who Shagged Me* was rated as a 12 certificate. That means children of 12 and 13 don't find the word offensive. If they are able to go to the cinema and watch a film with the word in the title, how can it be so offensive?'

Tell her to get stuffed

When Wiltshire resident Mary Kelly kept seeing schoolchildren damaging her fence as they climbed into her garden to retrieve footballs, she eventually reached the end of her tether. She emailed a letter of complaint to the local school, St John's, and sat back and waited for the school to respond to her complaints.

Imagine her surprise, then, when the school's headmaster replied, saying, 'Tell her to get stuffed.' This gaffe came about because Mrs Kelly had sent the original email to both the headmaster – Patrick Hazlewood – and to the school's bursar, Barry Worth. Hazlewood thought his reply was going directly and solely to

Worth's email account. Instead, it went straight to 62-year-old Mrs Kelly.

Hazlewood's response might have been intended for Worth's eyes only but it still constituted a rather aggressive response to a complaint from a retired lady. He explained later that his anger was the result of his growing frustration over delays to plans to build a new school building – delays caused in part by opposition to the plans from Duck Meadows residents such as Mrs Kelly. His 'get stuffed' comment was written just 48 hours before the district council was due to decide whether those plans would get the red light.

'My response was in the light of all the difficulties caused by these people,' he said of the opponents to the plans. 'I did not feel very happy and it was a light-hearted comment to Barry Worth to tell her to get stuffed. These people [objectors to the St John's new school] have cost us the best part of £1 million in delays and then we are told we have to mend a fence.'

This was not the first time that Hazlewood had attracted the attention of the media. In 2005, he decided to scrap homework for pupils at his school. He compared the idea of home-work to 'a dinosaur'. Looks like he could do with swotting up on how email works.

We now have a major clear-up operation

Email, we have long been told, will eliminate the need for traditional offices. The much-vaunted 'paperless' office will quickly become the way of the future. So it is not without irony that an emailed request for, of all things, a good old-fashioned filing cabinet managed to bring a whole region's computer system to a standstill.

An unnamed woman who worked for the NHS in Cambridgeshire wrote an email requesting a filing cabinet and a swivel chair for her office. She intended to send the message to a small group of email addresses but she accidentally sent the request to 5,000 people working in surgeries, hospitals and offices all over Cambridgeshire.

Many of those who received the email decided to have a bit of fun and fired off some joke replies asking for hat stands and tin cans – oh, the unbridled wit of the office-email joker! Others forwarded on the original message to friends.

Before long, with these messages bouncing back and forward, the county's NHS computer system was more clogged up than a chain-smoking, fry-up-guzzling patient's arteries.

As the local servers buckled under the strain, IT bosses had to beg employees across the region to stop using email. 'Critical systems relating to patient care and finance have been damaged,' said one in typical IT jargon. He then got so terrified by the scale of the problem that he reverted to everyday English, adding, 'We now have a major clear-up operation.'

As the woman who sent the original email squirmed with embarrassment, health partnership managing director Keith Spencer said, 'It was a fairly innocuous request for a chair. What developed was some light-hearted, but inappropriate banter across the network. It resulted in a significant increase in network traffic which had the effect of slowing down the infrastructure. We want to learn from what happened and get the message across to staff that our network is a business system and should not be misused.'

It completely crashed my computer

Giles Elliott was chief executive of Bridgewell, the firm he had helped to form, but in August 2006 he decided to leave to pursue new options. Keen to let his numerous contacts in the world of finance know of his exciting new plans, Elliott sent a 'round robin' email to all of his contacts. However, a computer glitch meant the email got caught on a loop which meant that the email was sent out again and again.

Over 1,000 people were on the address list for this email and each was sent hundreds and hundreds of the same email, which meant many of their computers crashed. The address list included City superwoman Nicola Horlick, the Korean Embassy and Central Parking Systems. One recipient commented, 'It completely crashed my computer. I had a full screen of Giles Elliott. There were hundreds and hundreds.' Having sorted the problem on his computer, the same recipient found that he had to also reboot his Blackberry. 'It has been very infuriating,' he snapped.

Journalist Martin Waller was also on the list

and treated readers of *The Times* to daily updates on the fiasco.

'Giles Elliott, former chief executive of Bridgewell, has retired,' wrote Waller on day one. 'I know this and, if you're in his enormous contacts book, you'll have been told it several dozen times as well, because Elliott has had a Bad E-Mail day... This could go on for some time.'

On day two, Waller reported, 'A friend copied his reply to Elliott's entire address book. My score yesterday: another 12 from Elliott and 25 from his mate. And still they proliferate.'

Then came day three. 'The number of messages informing his City chums that he is retiring from Bridgewell is actually rising daily and some of his thousands of other City contacts are losing their sense of humour. I finally reach him to ask him to do something. "The e-mails still seem to be continuing," says Elliott. You bet.'

By day four, humour was in even shorter supply: 'It is now Day 4 of the Giles Elliott e-mail fiasco, and it has ceased to be amusing. Yesterday the wretched things were still arriving, along with increasingly desperate messages from other recipients pleading with Elliott to please,

please, not send it again. These only go into the same loop and go round and round to everyone again. My inbox crashed six times yesterday.

'I have managed to get any further messages blocked automatically. This means Giles will never be able to e-mail me again, on any subject. And after this week, that's no bad thing.'

Meanwhile, Elliott was desperately trying to stop the emails in their tracks. 'I am spending a lot of time on the phone to Bangladesh, or wherever their call centre is,' he pleaded. 'I am hoping that the thing will die a death eventually.' Which it did.

However, in October 2006, a similar problem broke out at US investment bank State Street Advisors. Reporting on this story, Martin Waller allowed himself one final dig at Elliott. He wrote, 'One recalls Giles Elliott, former head of Bridgewell, whose retirement message went into a similar loop and virtually shut down the City's e-mail network in August. Come to think of it, I haven't heard much from Giles of late...'

You will die in seven days

Hell might have no fury like a woman scorned but the fury of a sacked male employee can come pretty close. David Lennon was 16 years old when he got a part-time job with the insurance firm Domestic & General Group. However, the teenager was fired in 2003.

The following year, he decided that revenge would be sweet. Lennon used an email 'bombing' program called Avalanche to bombard his former bosses with a series of hoax emails. Quite sinister emails, as it turned out: the messages contained a series of warnings, including one from the hit horror film *The Ring* that read: 'You will die in seven days' and another that read: 'Everyone will suffer'. Some of the emails purported to be sent from the company's employees and others were made to look as if they had been sent by Microsoft boss Bill Gates.

Between 31 January and 4 February 2004, five million of these emails were sent to his former employers until the mail servers and routers crashed at the firm's offices in Britain, Germany, Spain and France. This cost the company an estimated £30,000.

The Metropolitan Police's computer crime unit investigated and within months they had traced the emails to Lennon's home. However, it took three years to bring Lennon to justice. In November 2005, a judge ruled that Lennon had no case to answer. District Judge Kenneth Grant had said that the law which concerns unauthorised modification of data had not been breached, as emails sent to a server configured to receive emails could not be classified as unauthorised.

The prosecutors appealed and, in May 2006, judges at the Royal Courts of Justice sent the case back to the Magistrates Court, saying Judge Grant 'was not right to state there was no case to answer'. Mr Justice Jack said the judge should consider 'what answer Mr Lennon might have expected if he had asked D&G' before starting the email bombing.

On 24 August 2006, Lennon became the first person to be convicted of a 'denial of service' offence under the 1990 Computer Misuse Act when he pleaded guilty to an offence under Section 3 of the Act for 'causing an unauthorised modification to a computer'. Detective Constable Bob Burls, who led the investigation, said, 'This was a malicious and premeditated email attack by the offender on a former employer that resulted in financial loss and disruption to business.'

Wimbledon Youth Court sentenced Lennon – by now 19 – to a two-month curfew. He was also fitted with an electronic tag. Lennon – dubbed the 'five million email nit' by the *Sun* – got off lightly: he could have been jailed for up to five years.

However, just as Lennon got off lightly, the same could be said of his employers. As online experts commented after his conviction, Lennon was a 'rank amateur' in the email-bombardment stakes when compared to racketeers who use bombardment to extort money from businesses. They identify companies that depend on the internet for their business and then bombard them with emails before offering to stop the email attack if the company pays them a protection fee.

Can you arrange a time for this asshole to come in?

The members-only Monte's club in Knights-bridge is owned by the Hyatt and part-run by celebrity chef Jamie Oliver. You would have thought that millionaire Jason Gissing was exactly the sort of person that Monte's would want as a member. However, he says he asked a number of times for a tour of the venue without success. He also said he suffered 'unpleasant' treatment at the venue's reception.

He sent a series of emails to the club, complaining of what had happened. Finally, manager Patricia Cusack snapped and wrote an email to her deputy which read: 'Amanda, can you arrange a time for this asshole to come in. Weekends at 8pm are no good for anyone – he obviously wants to make a night of it.' Unfortunately, she accidentally sent the angry message not to her deputy but to Gissing.

Gissing responded by forwarding the correspondence to some of his friends and it quickly circulated around the world. Cusack got a ticking-off from the Hyatt hotel chain and admitted the whole experience was very stressful. Gissing was subsequently offered membership of the Harrington Club in nearby South Kensington.

I just want the whole thing to go away so I can get on with my job

Reports of my death have been greatly exaggerated. That's what secretary Natalie Francisco could have said as she became embroiled in an email disaster in March 2001. The episode was sparked when a personnel executive at Herbert Smith – the London law firm where Francisco worked – decided it might be funny to send a joke email around staff pretending that Francisco had been murdered. The message expressed no regret at the death of a member of staff, nor any condolences for her family or friends. Instead, it coldly listed the temporary staff that would stand in for her.

Many of the staff believed the email was true and some of them were so shocked by the callous way the news was broken that they forwarded the email to friends and other contacts. The profession's leading journal *Legal Week* received copies too. It was very embarrassing for Herbert Smith.

Not that everyone who saw it was so morally outraged. One lawyer responded saying, 'I hope you signed her leaving card. Do you think one of the partners made a lame speech as her body made its final jerky exit towards the afterlife? It's a tough world and those lawyers are hardly the most sympathetic members of the global community, are they?'

Francisco was, of course, making no journey towards the afterlife. But you can imagine her shock when she first heard of the email. 'No one likes to read about their own murder,' she said. 'I was deeply upset by what happened and still can't believe that this message was sent. I just want the whole thing to go away so I can get on with my job.'

A spokesman for Herbert Smith said, 'It was a rather silly thing to do, but it did not contain obscene material or refer to clients. We will use it to tighten up our email policy. The lawyers involved will get an extremely serious talking-to.'

Can we go for a real fit busty blonde this time?

Adam Dowdney was once a partner at the 200-year-old law firm Charles Russell, which specialises in big-money City deals. He went to a posh boarding school in Devon and is a keen cricket player. His job at the firm – which he had joined four years previously – earned him an estimated £100,000 a year. So you would imagine he was a pretty sharp, with-it kind of guy.

However, when the firm's black secretary Rachel Walker handed in her resignation to the firm in 2001, Dowdney marked the occasion with an absolute howler of an email disaster. Just hours after Walker announced her resignation, Dowdney emailed his colleague Clive Hopewell to discuss her replacement and wrote: 'Can we go for a real fit busty blonde this time? She can't be any more trouble and at least it would provide some entertainment!!'

Somehow, Walker saw this email and complained to the head of the firm's human resources department. Dowdney and Hopewell immediately wrote letters of apology to Walker. In his letter, Dowdney described the email as a 'senseless and thoughtless joke' and expressed the wish that they could put the incident behind them. Hopewell called the email a 'childish joke' and said he hoped that it would not 'sour a good working relationship'. He offered to buy Walker lunch so they could discuss it further.

However, Walker was in no mood to let the matter pass so easily. She was so distraught by seeing the email that she could not sleep at night and her doctor signed her off work for a month. She also decided to sue for sex and race discrimination. The media leaped on to this story and the usual race-relations groups were quoted. At least Dowdney was going to be provided with some entertainment now, though perhaps not in the form he had hoped for in his email.

In her statement, Walker said, 'I was very upset by these e-mails and find the content and tone both racist and sexist... I felt very uncomfortable working at Charles Russell. Being in the office became unbearable.'

In the end, the case was settled out of court with Walker receiving £10,000 in compensation. However, the ramifications of the case were profound. They highlighted the fact that employees who believe they have a claim against an employer have the right to be given all emails relating to them.

One step up from the jokes on seaside postcards

David Pennington and Rupert Beverley faced the ultimate sanction available to their bosses when they were caught sending smutty jokes around their workplace via email. There was, it transpired, actually a ring of people involved in sending jokey emails around at Holset Engineering in Huddersfield. However, Pennington and Beverley were judged to have been the most prolific emailers in the ring. This judgement followed a three-week investigation that was sparked when one of the ring's emails was accidentally sent to a worker who complained to the bosses.

The pair were fired, immediately cried 'unfair dismissal' and took their case to an industrial tribunal in November 2000. There, Catherine Prest represented Holset. She argued, 'The company's major issues about it all were the content of the material being sent and the quantity.' When asked to describe the level of naughtiness in the jokey emails, she described it as 'one step up from the sort of jokes you used to find on traditional seaside postcards'.

Pennington and Beverley insisted they did not know they were doing anything wrong but the company countered that there was a clear policy on such matters. The tribunal rejected the pair's claims of wrongful dismissal.

The people who were sacked are not layabouts who spend all day surfing the net for dirty jokes

The same fate has befallen other people who have forwarded a few jokey emails round their workplace. Insurance giant Royal & Sun Alliance sacked 10 workers and suspended 90 others in 2001 when some saucy comedy emails were found to be circulating among its staff. The emails included a cartoon of Bart Simpson flashing his private parts at his naked sister Lisa. His mum Marge was also featured performing a sex act on another character from *The Simpsons*. Also included were images of *Muppets* characters including Kermit the frog and Fozzy Bear getting down and dirty.

There was also an email showing an aroused donkey chasing a man, and another that showed a Mastercard credit card with the text doctored to give the card a rude meaning. Also passed around email accounts at the company's Liverpool headquarters was a spoof Ali G interview.

A spokesman said, 'The implication that this is simply about some bad-taste Bart Simpson cartoon is wholly wrong. It goes well beyond that. As far as I am aware, no one who has been through the disciplinary procedure has seriously contested the fact that the material they have been caught with is unacceptable. It is important that we maintain the standards that our employees and customers would expect of us.'

Union leaders immediately warned that they might consider legal action against the company. 'The people who were sacked are not layabouts who spend all day surfing the net for dirty jokes,' said one. 'Some of them have been here for 10 or 15 years and never put a foot wrong. They have got families to support and mortgages to pay. If they had cracked a joke by the photocopier or passed a stupid cartoon round the desks, they would still have a job. But just because they used email, the same trivial thing becomes a sacking offence.'

All those suspended were allowed to return to work, some of them after receiving official warnings.

Jaguar will not tolerate this

The Royal & Sun Alliance case seemed to prompt similar incidents elsewhere in Britain. Within months, car giants Jaguar had suspended 11 workers from its plant in Halewood, Merseyside, because of a controversial email. A further 19 workers were also questioned at the plant, which made the X-type car known as the 'baby Jag'.

The email in question – the precise contents of which are unknown – was discovered when it was forwarded on to Jaguar's parent company in the US. A spokesman said, 'It is something, obviously, that Jaguar will not tolerate and we have issued warnings about such action in the past.'

Even though Jaguar would not tolerate it, it happened again within months when staff at the company's paint shop in Castle Bromwich in Birmingham were busted while circulating an email depicting Snow White having sex with the seven dwarves. One member of staff lost his job in the aftermath of this and a company spokesperson reiterated, 'Jaguar will not tolerate this.'

There are a lot of people deleting email today

Meanwhile, Ford was investigating a potential porn-ring at its Dagenham plant. It was alleged that some workers there had spent up to four hours each day visiting porn sites, illicitly using the password of a manager to gain access to the internet. Ford announced an investigation and suspended three workers on full pay.

Staff were subsequently given a two-week amnesty to delete all pornographic material from their computer terminals – or face the chop. It was announced that, following the amnesty, spot-checks would be undertaken on staff's computers. This led to much hurried deletion among Ford workers, with one admitting, 'We have never seen anything like it. There are a lot of people deleting email and other materials today.'

They were sacked for playing games on computers

In December 2002, British Nuclear Fuels – which had earlier suspended nine staff for allegedly distributing the same Bart Simpson email as the doomed Royal Sun & Alliance workers – was a company on top-level alert.

With the countdown to the war in Iraq making the threat of terrorist attacks on the UK more likely, staff were told to be extra-vigilant at nuclear power plants. That vigilance took an unexpected turn when 12 workers were fired for abusing its email systems and for playing games on the company's computers.

BNFL said, 'There has been disciplinary action against employees for abuse of our email system. They were sacked for playing games on computers. None breached confidentiality or accessed material of an offensive or pornographic nature.'

Dude, she wants some of that double penetration action

In 2003, the Christmas quiz in the legal journal

Legal Business included the following question: 'Which Clifford Chance associate was sacked for overt references to "spit roasting" in an email accidentally sent to senior management at Slaughter and May?'

The answer was Patrick Smith but we need to know more than that, don't we?

On 30 July, Smith – who was a junior lawyer at law firm Clifford Chance – was one of 30 recipients of an email invitation to the leaving-drinks party of another lawyer, Venn King of the spectacularly named law firm Slaughter and May. When Smith replied, he included a reference to a female lawyer the pair both knew. It read: 'Dude, [name of female lawyer] wants some of that double penetration action, so let me know when you and the old horse fat are around.'

What a pair of studs, eh? However, Smith did not just send the email to King, he accidentally hit 'reply all' and sent it to all 30 people on the original round-robin list. Inevitably, it was then forwarded on to friends of some of the 30 people and before long was being read worldwide.

When the email came to the attention of his managers, Smith was suspended from work while an internal inquiry was set up. Smith had not long since moved from Australia to England to try and make it big in law. This can't have helped his chances.

I went to a dry cleaners at lunch and they said it would cost £4 to remove ketchup stains

One day in 2005, secretary Jenny Amner was lunching with her boss Richard Phillips in the staff canteen at City firm Baker & McKenzie. During the lunch, Amner accidentally spilled some ketchup on her boss's suit. This was a rather silly mistake to make – but not half as silly as the one that her boss was about to make.

He wrote an email to his secretary, demanding she pay for the bill to remove the ketchup stain. With the subject line 'Ketchup trousers', his email read: 'Hi Jenny, I went to a dry cleaners at lunch and they said it would cost £4 to remove ketchup stains. If you cd let me have the cash today, that wd be much appreciated. Thanks Richard.'

When Mrs Amner did not immediately respond, Phillips followed up, leaving a Post-It note on her desk, reminding her of his request for the £4.

However, Mrs Amner had been slow in responding to his email because she had been off work following the death of her mother, Polly.

On returning to work, the grieving Mrs Amner saw red when she found Phillips's email and follow-up note. She replied to her boss's email with the following stinging message: 'I must apologise for not getting back to you straight away but due to my mother's sudden illness, death and funeral I have had more pressing issues than your £4.

'I apologise again for accidentally getting a few splashes of ketchup on your trousers. Obviously your financial need as a senior associate is greater than mine as a mere secretary.

'Having already spoken to and shown your email and Anne-Marie's note to various partners, lawyers and trainees, they kindly offered to do a collection to raise the £4. I however declined their kind offer but should you feel the urgent need for the £4 it will be on my desk this afternoon. Jenny.'

This was stinging enough, but Amner copied all of the office's 250 staff in on her reply. One of the staff recalled, 'She copied it to the whole floor and everyone was in stitches. She had come into work this morning to find a Post-It chasing her for the £4 after having the funeral the day before.'

Very quickly, some of the staff at the firm forwarded the email to City contacts and pretty soon the email was pinging around the financial community.

There, it provoked much discussion on website discussion forums. Sentiments of support for Phillips were thin on the ground. Like all good snowballing emails, the message was soon circulating around the world and Phillips was gathering himself a reputation as a mean tightwad, while Amner was collecting supportive messages from around the world.

The media loved the story and Phillips was quickly dubbed 'the ketchup meanie' while the affair was – somewhat predictably – called 'KETCHUPGATE'. It was picked up by media outlets across the world, prompting the *Agence France Presse* to note that Mr Phillips was 'on the verge of becoming a public hate figure … after appearing to show appalling meanness'.

Even the *Daily Mail*'s stuffy right-wing columnist Simon Heffer had a kick at the ketchup klutz. He stormed, 'Well-heeled solicitor Richard Phillips has, quite rightly, become a national figure of fun after sending his secretary, Jenny Amner, an email demanding £4 to cover the costs of cleaning a ketchup stain off his trousers. Given the legal profession's legendary greed, expect this man's bosses to promote him. I'm only amazed that he didn't also send Ms Amner an additional bill for his valuable time sending the email.'

Sunday Times columnist India Knight also weighed in behind Amner: 'If I were Baker & McKenzie, I would give her a pay rise,' she wrote.

Phillips did, however, receive support from blogger Harry Phibbs, who wrote on the Social Affairs Unit website. He said that the whole affair stank of envy and was symptomatic of widely held but wrong attitudes towards the rich. 'The poor are not enriched by despising and humiliating the successful,' he stormed. However, he managed to calm down enough to comfort himself that: 'I am not suggesting this will lead to the downfall of capitalism.' Thank the Lord for that!

The ketchup manufacturer Heinz took

advantage of the publicity by offering advice on stain removal: 'Vinegar diluted with water is an easy home remedy.' Great publicity for the tomato titans!

As the story gained legs, a spokesperson for Phillips's firm said, 'We confirm we are aware of the incident and subsequent email exchange. This is a private matter between two members of staff that clearly got out of hand. We are investigating so as to resolve it as amicably as we can. As I am sure you understand, we respect the privacy of our staff and make it a policy not to comment on individuals to the media.'

Phillips was said by close friends to be 'devastated' by his public humiliation. He resigned from his £150,000-a-year job in the aftermath of the episode. The firm claimed that he had planned to quit 'long before' the ketchup controversy but the story still seemed to end very unhappily for him. However, given that his areas of expertise were supposed to be IT and media, it is strangely appropriate that those two forces combined to bring about his humiliation.

I'd love to do this. I can't think of anything I'd rather spend my weekend doing!

This story was sent to me during my research for this book. The sender has asked to have his details kept secret so let's call him Jake and say that he works for a retail company in the north of England.

'Jake' takes up the story: 'The head of human resources at a previous firm I worked at was known as a bit of a boring old do-gooder. She regularly emailed the whole staff list and asked us to take part in various worthy causes: recycling ink cartridges, sponsoring her niece in her sponsored walk and so on and so forth.

'She became something between a standing joke and a celebrated pest because of her emails. Very few people ever helped her but we all had a good laugh whenever her emails popped up. One Christmas, she emailed round asking whether any of us were willing to spend a weekend visiting old people's homes across the county. She explained that we would be distributing books and video tapes to the homes and "might have to get into the Christmas spirit

44

by singing to the residents/playing parlour games with them".

'This was too priceless to let pass without a laugh. So I wrote a message in response, saying, sarcastically, "I'd love to do this. I can't think of anything I'd rather spend my weekend doing!" I intended only to forward this message to a mate who works in another department but, instead of clicking the Forward icon, I instead clicked the 'reply' icon and sent the message direct to the do-gooder herself!

'Needless to say, I couldn't exactly go up to her and say, "That message was just a joke, I don't really want to do it." And so it was that this mug spent an entire weekend trudging round old people's home after old people's home, singing carols and giving presents to a load of miserable old sods.

'I'd love to say that the experience proved to be enjoyable or rewarding in some way. It wasn't. It was the most boring weekend of my life and actually made me wish I had gone Christmas shopping with the missus. I no longer send jokes over email.'

I sent the most apologetic, pleading-for-mercy note of my life

Our penultimate bad day at the office centres on marketing executive Alex Clark, who made a similar silly mistake when mocking his company's chief executive in an email. Clark's boss was unable to attach a document to an email and Clark sent a message to friends and colleagues poking fun at this fact.

He realised he had accidentally sent it to the boss himself. 'I sent the most sincere, apologetic, pleading-for-mercy note of my life,' he says.

I bet he did. Fortunately, it did the trick and he kept his job.

I work somewhere else now

The final word on workplace calamities goes to 'Neil', who responded to a BBC plea for stories of email disasters to tell his own sorry tale.

'I took a "sick" day once and sent an email the next day boasting to my friends about the cause: lots of beer! Except the email went to my whole department by mistake instead! I work somewhere else now.'

CHAPTER THREE

WESTMINSTER WOES

O n 11 September 2001, the world sat trans-
fixed with horror in front of its TV screens.
As we watched the twin towers of the World
Trade Center burning and saw people jump to
their deaths from the upper floors, many
thoughts went through our heads. Who did this?
How could anyone do this? How many people are
going to die? How will America respond? But, for
one person, other thoughts sprang to mind.

This is a good day to bury bad news

Jo Moore was the special adviser and personal

spin doctor to Transport Secretary Stephen Byers. As the towers were burning, she emailed colleagues suggesting that it was a good day to bury bad news. Certainly, a suspicious number of government announcements were made that afternoon, including the controversial appointment of Gavyn Davies as BBC chairman, the abandonment of the planned national athletic stadium at Picketts Lock, the go-ahead for a new plant at Sellafield and an increase in payments to councillors.

Similarly, the following month, on the day that military strikes against Afghanistan began, Byers's department announced that it was to put Railtrack into receivership. Everyone involved in these announcements insists that their timing was entirely unrelated to events in Lower Manhattan and Afghanistan. Indeed, a Downing Street spokesman said that an announcement about asylum figures was delayed from its original scheduled date in mid-September to avoid accusations that the government were seeking to bury bad news.

Which brings us back to Jo Moore and her email. On 8 October 2001, Moore's 'bury bad news' memo was leaked and calls for her to quit began immediately. Conservative Party chairman David Davis called her 'tasteless beyond belief' and the press was quick to hurl abuse at her. For four weeks, our papers had been filled with little other than talk of terrorism, anthrax, dirty bombs and funerals. As we adjusted to this new threat, it was almost with a sense of relief that we greeted a good, domestic political scandal.

Downing Street was the first to defend her, a spokesman saying that, while she had committed an 'error of judgement', the whole affair should be 'kept in perspective'. However, political rumour had it that influential party members were privately demanding her immediate dismissal. Then Moore herself spoke, saying, 'I would like to sincerely apologise for the offence I have caused. It was wrong to send the email and I accept responsibility for doing so.'

The following day, Prime Minister Tony Blair spoke about the affair in the House of Commons. Moore's email was 'horrible, stupid and wrong', he said. Wrists had been slapped, public apologies made and it seemed that everyone was ready to draw a line under it and accept that lessons had been learned and that we should all just move on.

However, within five months, it appeared that not everyone had learned their lesson. On Valentine's Day 2002, two national newspapers reported that Jo Moore was once again seeking to sneak out some bad news on a busy news day. Although this time she had the sense not to make her suggestion via cyberspace, it was again an email that brought the whole affair to light.

The newspapers alleged that Moore had seen the day of Princess Margaret's funeral as another opportunity to bury bad news. The reports suggested that Moore had advised Stephen Byers to release embarrassing rail statistics on the day of the funeral. They also claimed that, when Byers's press chief Martin Sixsmith learned of her plans, he sent a fuming email to her saying, 'Dear Jo, There is no way I will allow this department to make any substantive announcements next Friday. Princess

Margaret is being buried on that day. I will absolutely not allow anything else to be.'

By 9am on the day these reports were published, Moore had issued an angry denial of the stories, which she described as 'complete and utter lies'. By the end of the day, the Prime Minister's official spokesman Godric Smith and the Leader of the Commons Robin Cook had both backed her denial.

No sooner had these denials been made, than reports of a different email emerged in which Sixsmith had told Byers, 'You spoke about possibly making this announcement on Friday. We should not do it on Friday, as that is the day on which Princess Margaret is being buried. There are too many connotations to the word "buried" for us to do anything on that day.'

There was fury in government circles that they had denied an email that did exist, albeit in not the same terms as initially reported. Moore and Sixsmith both resigned from their jobs. Moore had quickly become infamous and appeared at number 59 on the voting for the *100 Worst Britons* TV programme. She is now a teacher.

The people taking over from Pam Warren... basically are they Tories?

But Moore's departure from Byers's department did not mean that the department had learned its lesson about being indiscreet when using online communications. Just four months after the royal funeral scandal, another email emerged from the department to cause all concerned huge embarrassment.

Again, tragedy was at the heart of this new crisis. On 5 October 1999, some 31 people had died when a train passed a red signal and collided with another train near Paddington station at 8.11am. The tragedy had shaken and moved the nation, as did the courage of the survivors, most notably Pam Warren who had suffered horrific injuries when a fireball engulfed her carriage.

Warren spent months in hospital but emerged as the articulate spokesperson for the Paddington Survivors' Group. The group highlighted the continuing dangers of railway policies and campaigned for more to be done to make the railways safer. She was easily recognisable because of the clear plastic mask she had to wear to ensure that the scar tissue on her face healed.

By 2002, her campaign had gathered much momentum and Warren was proving an embarrassment to the government, especially in May of that year when during an interview with the *Daily Mail* she accused Stephen Byers of misleading Parliament over the future of Railtrack. So, when in June reports emerged suggesting that the government were trying to smear her, there was widespread outrage. The reports claimed that a special adviser to Byers had sent an email to probe Warren's background and political allegiances.

Once again, it all kicked off. Conservative Transport Spokeswoman Theresa May roared, 'It's about this whole culture of spin that is there at the heart of the government. Anybody who stands up and says what from their experience they know to be true and happens to be against the government, the government tries to come down on them like a ton of bricks.'

The Liberal Democrats' Don Foster added, 'This is an appalling and inappropriate way for a government department to behave.'

The tabloids sensed blood and were full of indignation. As for Warren herself, she said that, if such an email had been sent, then it would reveal 'a nasty and spiteful nature within the government'.

Once the story was properly investigated, it emerged that the initial reports were somewhat exaggerated. The truth was that an email had been sent by a Byers aide to Labour headquarters. However, it did not concern Warren but was actually enquiring whether those due to succeed her at the head of the Paddington Survivors' Group had links with any political party. The most damning passages were: 'The people taking over from Pam Warren... basically are they Tories?' and 'They seem to have an anti-SB [Stephen Byers] agenda and we want to find out what lies behind it.'

All this was too late to save Byers who had quit at the end of May 2002 after a series of troubles had made his position untenable. His successor, Alistair Darling, distanced himself from the emails sent by Byers's aide, saying he 'strongly disapproves of the fact that this inquiry was made and has made it clear that it must stop immediately'.

What New Labour hoped would be the final word on the Byers files went to spin doctor Alastair Campbell who said, 'There are obviously lessons that government must and will learn from this affair.' Indeed. Don't let political advisers use email could be one of them.

The legacy of Jo Moore's email continued to haunt Tony Blair, however. The phrase 'a good day to bury bad news' has entered the political lexicon and continues to be hurled at New Labour whenever possible. In 2006, for instance, it was revealed that Tony Blair had been questioned by police as part of the cash for peerages investigation.

This was a very embarrassing moment for Blair, nine years after he arrived in Downing Street promising to clean up politics after years of Tory sleaze. The news that he had been questioned was released on the same day as Lord Stevens published his report into the death of Princess Diana. The coincidence of the two announcements was not lost on the press, who rounded on Blair and accused him of timing his announcement to 'bury bad news'.

Opposition figures had a pop too. Chris Grayling, a Tory spokesman, said, 'Five years after Labour launched the concept of burying bad news, Mr Blair's spin doctors are back to their old tricks.'

On that week's edition of BBC1's *Have I Got News For You*, Ian Hislop sarcastically praised Blair saying his main ability was 'being good at burying bad news'.

Obviously I'm not prone to leak secrets left, right and centre... but this needed to get out

Anyone who read a headline about 'The blonde who dropped a bombshell on Blair' might have been expecting a 'kiss and tell' story about the Prime Minister. But the story of Katharine Gun is more of a 'print and tell' story – and one that blew the lid off the shenanigans behind the scenes during the run-up to the Iraq war.

Gun was a translator who worked for the government's GCHQ in Cheltenham. Her job was to work through and translate long transcripts of interceptions that the government had picked up while eavesdropping. The content of these transcripts was often quite dull, to say the least. But not on 31 January 2003 – the day that changed Gun's life.

On that morning, Gun received an email from Frank Koza, who was the head of regional targets at the US National Security Agency. The email was requesting British help in an alleged plot to bug UN delegates from Angola, Chile, Cameroon, Guinea, Pakistan and Mexico. These six countries were, it was deemed, the ones that could swing the vote for a UN resolution approving of war in Iraq.

Gun described how she was deeply shocked by the email and went and sat in the toilet, to try and take in the enormity of what she had just read. She believed that, if the email became public knowledge, war in Iraq could be averted. She spent the following weekend mulling over whether she should leak the message or not.

She decided to act and printed off the email and passed it on to a friend. The printout found its way to Yvonne Ridley, the newspaper journalist who had recently been taken hostage by the Taliban in Afghanistan. Ridley then passed it on to the *Observer*'s Martin Bright. After rigorously checking its veracity, the *Observer* printed the story.

GCHQ staff were interrogated over what they knew about the leak. Gun eventually admitted that she was responsible and she was arrested by the Special Branch and charged under the Official Secrets Act. She commented, 'I'm just baffled that in the 21st century we as human beings are still dropping bombs on each other as a means to resolve issues.' However, when she came to trial, Gun who received widespread support from many figures – including the actor Sean Penn who described her as a 'hero of the human spirit' – found that the case against her was dropped because, many believe, even more sensitive facts might have come out.

She emerged from court with a bunch of roses and called her mother to tell her the good news. She insisted she regretted nothing about the episode, as she told a news conference, 'Obviously I'm not prone to leak secrets left, right and centre... but this needed to get out, the public deserved to know what was going on at the time.

'I was pretty horrified and I felt that the British intelligence services were being asked to do something that would undermine the whole UN democratic processes.'

Let me know if I can be of service, your pleasure is my purpose

There was nothing illegal about Cherie Blair allowing Peter Foster to help her purchase two flats. Nor was there anything immoral about the arrangement. However, when Blair denied that Foster had helped her buy the flats, she opened the door for all her critics in Fleet Street to shout, 'You're totally busted!' while waving printouts of emails in her face.

The scandal that rocked Downing Street in 2002 started when the *Mail On Sunday* claimed Cherie Blair had allowed Peter Foster – who has been dubbed an 'international man of mischief' and 'the greatest conman of all time' among other things – to help her buy two flats in Bristol, where her son Euan was at university. Downing Street immediately denied the claim and stressed that Foster – the boyfriend of Carole Caplin, a close friend of the Blairs – was not a financial adviser to Blair.

Any hope that the story would die there was dashed when, just days later, the *Daily Mail* published emails that proved Foster and Blair had indeed combined during the purchase of the flats. Under the headline: CHERIE, A CROOK AND THE PROOF NUMBER 10 LIED, the paper published excerpts from a string of emails sent by Foster to Blair at her law chambers.

During the exchange, Blair said, 'You are a star, I have sent them [the mortgage forms] off', and later added, 'Thank you so much Peter, I appreciate that.' At another point, Foster talks about 'our agreement' and says, 'Let me know if I can be of service... as I tell Carole, your pleasure is my purpose (she hates that saying, hence the need to say it often enough and loud enough).' He later explained that he has 'put a rocket' under the letting agent for the properties. He also wrote, 'So do you buy two apartments or one? Buggered if I know, I'm just a bloody Australian.'

Naturally, the press went mad and hurled all manner of abuse at the Blairs who saved, it was claimed, £69,000 on the deal thanks to Foster's involvement. They also highlighted Foster's previous conviction for promoting fraudulent diet pills and his connection with former Page 3 model Samantha Fox. Foster remembers that, during this period, he was accused of everything from being a Mossad agent to being the father of twins he had never met and starting his business on drugs money.

Headlines during this period included THE LITANY OF LIES GOES ON; WATERS GO MURKIER STILL and TALES OF SHOWERS, SEX AND THE NUMBER 10 PLOT. In the *Mirror*, columnist Paul Routledge wrote, 'Not many conmen and their loves can rely on the PM's wife to rush to their aid... but most don't act on her behalf in a £500,000 property deal.'

After facing five days of flak, Cherie Blair decided to use a speech she was making at a charity function in a Westminster restaurant to apologise for the entire episode. In a speech reportedly written by Peter Mandelson and Alastair Campbell, an at times tearful Cherie sniffed, 'In view of all the controversy around me at the moment, I hope you do not mind me using this event to say a few words. I know I am in a very special position. I am the wife of the prime minister, I have an interesting job and a wonderful family, but I also know I am not superwoman.

'The reality of my daily life is that I am juggling a lot of balls in the air – some of you must have experienced that.'

She continued, 'Trying to be a good wife and mother, trying to be the prime ministerial consort at home and abroad and being a barrister, a charity worker. And sometimes some of the balls get dropped. There just aren't enough hours in the day.

'He was not my financial adviser, but I should not have allowed a situation to develop where Tony's spokesman said he played no part in the negotiations, and I take full responsibility for that.

'Obviously, if I had known the full details of Mr Foster's past, I would not have allowed myself to get into this situation.

'I am sorry if I have embarrassed anyone, but the people who know me well know that I would never want to harm anyone, least of all Tony, or the children, or the Labour government, or misuse my position in any way at all.

'Sometimes I feel I'd like to crawl away and hide but I will not and I have come here tonight to present you with your well-deserved awards and that's what I am going to do.'

The following morning, the Blairs tried to crawl away from the scandal when they cut all ties with Foster and paid off the fees he said he accrued during the negotiations. The Prime Minister also rejected growing opposition calls for a parliamentary inquiry into the saga. Characteristically, he also said he hoped everyone would 'move on'.

Robbie would like to recall the message 'Advantages of being Chinese'

In 2005, then Chancellor of the Exchequer Gordon Brown went on a trip to China. He saw Chinese business as vital to the UK and undertook the tour to attempt to improve relations. The four-day whirlwind tour included visits to Shanghai and Shenzen. He met key ministers and initiated a five-point plan for improved cooperation between the two countries.

Delighted with the success of the trip, Mr Brown

said, 'What we are seeing is an opening up of a broad and deep partnership, cooperation and engagement between Britain and China.'

So imagine his horror when, within months of the trip, one of his aides made a major email gaffe involving a silly joke about Chinese people.

You don't just stumble into a job in government press offices. Treasury press officer Robbie Browse was one of the geniuses of presentation and image that make the New Labour machinery so slick and impressive. However, even with all his expertise – and with his internet-related surname – he still managed to succumb to the perils of email.

One afternoon in January 2006, Browse composed a jokey email and intended to send it to friends. However, he accidentally sent it to 83 national newspaper journalists who are on his press list for major announcements. This list included the editors of the *Observer* and the *Sunday Telegraph* along with senior hacks from the *Daily Mail* and the *Mirror*.

The subject line of the email read: 'The advantages of being Chinese.' Attached to the email was an indecipherable jumble of shapes.

The message read: 'This is brilliant!!! If you cannot decipher anything, try pulling the corner of your eyes as if you were Chinese. It works!' When the reader pulls their eyes to alter their focus, then the jumble of shapes reads: 'No sex causes bad eyes'.

Just the sort of email that Brown would have hoped his aides would send out to leading journalists as he attempted to woo the Chinese, really. Within 240 seconds of the message being sent out, Browse had discovered his error. Such was his horror at his cock-up, he began to refer to himself in the third person, as he sent out a second email to the same list saying: 'Robbie would like to recall the message "Advantages of being Chinese".'

It is understood that Browse then confessed to his superiors what happened and faced a huge bollocking. Minutes later, another message was sent out by him. It read: 'Dear all. Please disregard the earlier email sent to the standard Treasury press list in error, and please accept my sincere apologies for any offence it has inadvertently caused. My job is to email out press notices and I regret that I have accidentally sent a personal email to you. Please accept my apologies again. Robbie Browse.'

Gordon Brown was then informed of the howler and a full investigation was mounted. It is not known what, if any, punishment Browse faced but a spokesman said, 'He's very apologetic and deeply regrets what he did', and that 'appropriate action is being taken'.

Meanwhile, newspaper journalists tried to find a Chinese authority to come up with a horrified quote. Unfortunately, the Chinese Embassy would not comment and a spokeswoman from London's Chinese Community Centre said that the email was obviously just a joke.

Browse's email had something of the Duke of Edinburgh about it. The Duke once talked about the 'slitty eyes' of the Chinese during a tour of the country. It's not known if he has an email account but, if he does, the potential comedy to be had from his great email disasters must be huge.

The final word on Browse's case must go to one of the recipients of his original email. The *Sunday Express* political editor Julia Hartley-Brewer wrote, 'Will we all be invited to your leaving party?'

The best is yet to come!

John McTernan sends out a daily email to Labour MPs to keep them abreast of current affairs. The man – dubbed 'Tony Blair's little helper' – often has a bit of fun at the expense of Conservative leader David Cameron. However, one day his email came back to haunt him.

'If you thought Cameron's conference speech was poor,' he sniggered, 'there are a few hints as to why this might be the case. Cameron: "The best is yet to come"; Charles Kennedy's Lib-Dem speech: "The best is yet to come".'

The email was seen by a journalist who quickly pointed out that Labour Party chair Hazel Blears had said at that very year's conference: 'We want a fourth term! The best, as they say, is yet to come!' Oops!

The dossier had been round the houses several times

Hundreds of emails emerged during the Hutton Inquiry into the death of Dr David Kelly, which was the first government hearing to request and publish email messages. Emails written by an unnamed witness – known only as Mr A – were read out during the inquiry. His emails complained that the Iraqi intelligence dossier was interfered with by 'spin merchants of this administration'. He also wrote in an email that the dossier had 'been round the houses several times' in order to 'strengthen certain political objectives'.

Also during the inquiry, emails sent by Tony Blair's chief of staff, Jonathan Powell, were read out. One warned that there was 'no imminent threat' posed by Iraq. Oh dear, how embarrassing!

These and other emails are now freely available for perusal by anyone who fancies a squint at the Public Record Office in Kew, which has been storing government emails since 2004.

My treatment says an awful lot about what is wrong with this country

Of course, many emails come to light without the Public Record Office having to get involved. Many of us enjoy having a good rant over email. Nicholas Faulkner used to work for the Home Office as a security consultant and his hobby horses included the price of houses, high taxation levels and mass immigration. He once sent an email to one of his superiors ranting about these topics and lost his job as a result.

There is – as you might suspect – a bit more to this story than that. The email that Faulkner sent ranting about the above matters was to none another than Tony Blair. In the message, Faulkner was also asking Blair for a bit of a favour. He wanted to know if the Prime Minister could fast-track his application for a US visa.

In short, he was saying to the PM: I'm a discontent, get me out of here! As a result of his email, he did indeed get out of here – but 'here' was not the UK. Rather it was his job with the Home Office. When his bosses got wind of his attempt to get his visa fast-tracked, his £90,000-per-year contract with the Immigration and Nationality Directorate in Croydon was terminated. 'He has misused confidential information for personal purposes in breach of contract, which was terminated,' said a Home Office spokesman.

Faulkner was fuming at this and his anger was made all the more intense by the fact that his neighbour in the office was Abid Javid. Mr Javid had previously been revealed to be a member of an Islamic group which, in the wake of the 7 July bombings, Blair had tried to ban. The Hizb ut-Tahrir group, of which Javid was a senior member, refuses to condemn suicide bombers. Despite Blair's opposition to the group, Javid had managed to keep his job at the Home Office.

Faulkner was disgusted by the fact that he'd lost his job because of a simple email while Javid kept his. He told the *Mail On Sunday*, 'My treatment compared to that of Abid says an awful lot about what is wrong with this country and what is happening to democracy.'

You can't help thinking that, given his favourite email hobby horses and his apparent bitterness, Faulkner should be a star columnist for the *Mail On Sunday*.

However, writing in the *Mirror*, columnist Sue Carroll had no sympathy. 'He broke the first rule of office life,' she wrote, under the headline HE'S BEEN E-NAILED. 'Before computers, people wrote resignation letters, usually after lunch, which they took back in the cold light of day.

But, as Mr Faulkner has discovered, the "send" button is merciless.'

It is indeed – and very expensive too! In 2006, 78,000 internal emails, letters and memos were sent by Home Office employees via internal mail at a total cost of £1.62 million a year – or £20.83 for each message!

Loans for Sir

The cash-for-peerages affair began when it emerged that a number of large secret loans had swelled the Labour Party coffers before the 2005 general election, and that some of the lenders had subsequently been nominated for peerages. Scotland Yard launched an investigation into the affair, to see whether any laws had been broken.

During the investigation – led by Metropolitan Police Assistant Commissioner John Yates – the police unearthed an embarrassing email sent by Matt Carter, who was then Labour Party general secretary, to a number of Labour officials. The email was sent in April 2005, just two days after Labour landed a £2.3 million loan from tycoon David Garrard.

It had recently emerged in the media that the Conservatives were facing a probe over secret loans, which were said to be bankrolling their campaign. Carter sent the email to senior Labour officials, warning them not to have a pop at the Conservatives because Labour was 'taking loans too'. After all, it would be awful if a politician were open to charges of hypocrisy, wouldn't it?

The recipients of the email included Minister without Portfolio Alan Milburn, Matthew Taylor, then of the Downing Street policy unit, Philip Gould, who worked for Tony Blair, Jo Gibbons, the Downing Street director of events, and Spencer Livermore, who was a key adviser to Gordon Brown. The presence of Livermore on the list raised suspicions that Brown – who insists he knew nothing of the loans – might have known more about them than he was letting on.

The email came to public attention in December 2006, the week after Conservative MP Andrew Tyrie said in a speech, 'Gordon Brown fought like an alley cat to have a central role in Labour's election campaign. I find it surprising that a man like Brown, who is so obsessed with detail ... could have no interest at all in knowing how the £18 million Labour spent was raised.'

By the time the email story broke, Matt Carter had moved jobs and was working for a US polling company. Journalists called him, asking for an interview about the email. He failed to return their calls so they decided to email him instead. Again, there was no response. He had probably had just about enough of emailing for one lifetime.

Do you feel embarrassed at having benefited from positive discrimination?

In 2004, Sir Trevor McDonald agreed to attend a charity lunch and answer questions there during a 'turn the tables' session. The *Independent*'s mischievous Pandora diary column asked its readers to suggest a 'killer question' to be given to Sir Trevor at the lunch for Cancer Research. (A killer question for a cancer event? Isn't this already getting a little unfortunate?)

Tory MP Jonathan Sayeed emailed Pandora to

suggest they ask: 'Do you feel embarrassed at having benefited from positive discrimination?' The shit immediately hit the fan as Pandora published this email in the *Independent*. Race-relations groups kicked up an almighty storm, with one encouraging Sir Trevor to sue Sayeed. Even more gravely, heavyweight political commentators Richard Madeley and Judy Finnegan got involved, calling Sayeed 'crass' in their column in the *Express*.

Sayeed – whose father was Indian – quickly apologised saying, 'If I have caused any offence inadvertently, then I will of course apologise. With my family background, I am the last person to poke fun at someone who has achieved so much.' He added that he had meant to ask if Sir Trevor felt embarrassed about 'the allegation' that his colour had helped him succeed.

Sir Trevor rose above the whole controversy, insisting that Sayeed's original question was 'juvenile' rather than offensive. 'It would be nice to know how I've benefited from positive discrimination,' he added.

This was appalling timing by Sayeed, who

was already under investigation for taking American tourists – who had paid a company he co-owned for their trips – on tours around Westminster. (He was later suspended for this breach of parliamentary rules.) Sayeed's fellow Tory MP Boris Johnson had recently offended the people of Liverpool by publishing an article in *The Spectator*, the magazine he edited, that accused them of wallowing in a victim mentality. As Sayeed and Johnson grovelled for their mistakes, the party's leader Michael Howard must have already been kissing goodbye to any dreams of taking office.

Piss off – we're full!

However, these gaffes were as nothing compared to one that would subsequently break and leave the Tories red-faced. Ellenor Bland runs a clothes shop in Wootton Bassett in Wiltshire and lives in the village of Quemerford. In 2006, an email was sent from her account with a photograph of the white cliffs of Dover with a slogan painted on them that told foreigners: 'Piss off – we're full.'

It also included a highly controversial poem about immigration. In full, the poem read:

I cross ocean poor and broke
Take bus, see employment folk.
Nice man treat me good in there.
Say I need to see welfare.
Welfare say, 'You come no more, we send
*   cash right to your door.'*
Welfare cheques – they make you wealthy!
*   NHS – it keep you healthy!*
By and by, I got plenty money.
Thanks to you, British dummy!
Write to friends in motherland.
Tell them 'come fast as you can'.
They come in turbans and Ford trucks.
I buy big house with welfare bucks!
They come here, we live together.
More welfare cheques, it gets better!
Fourteen families, they moving in,
But neighbour's patience wearing thin.
Finally, white guy moves away.
Now I buy his house, then I say,
Find more aliens for house to rent.'
And in the yard I put a tent.

Everything is very good, and soon we own
the neighbourhood.
We have hobby, it's called breeding.
Welfare pay for baby feeding.
Kids need dentist? Wife need pills? We get
free! We got no bills!
Britain crazy! They pay all year, to keep
welfare running here.
We think UK darn good place.
Too darn good for the white man race!
If they no like us, they can scram.
Got lots of room in Pakistan!

Not a very pleasant poem. However, it was especially newsworthy because Bland doesn't just run a clothes shop – she was also a councillor for the Conservative Party!

Bland quickly distanced herself from the email. She told reporters, 'I haven't sent anything that I'm accused of sending. Someone else did. My email address is something that's used by my husband, too. It's not my personal email account.'

The newspapers delighted in pointing out the email was signed: 'Oh yes! Ellie!'

Nonetheless, Bland added, 'From what I remember of it, it was a very light-hearted poem. We have Asian friends and we work well together and all accept each other's different ways.'

This did nothing to stop the row and pretty soon one of Bland's Asian friends came forward to confirm that he found the poem offensive. Ala Uddin, who owns a restaurant and has known Bland for many years, said, 'This kind of poem can be damaging. It is wrong, and it should not be sent around as a joke.'

Edward Davey, the Liberal Democrat campaigns chief, said, 'It is totally unacceptable for elected representatives to be distributing this kind of material. Racism has absolutely no place in British politics and I am asking the CRE to advise on what further action can be taken.

'If David Cameron wants to retain any credibility, he must immediately take the strongest action against the person responsible. Despite Cameron's best PR efforts, the Conservative Party continues to contain some deeply unpleasant elements.'

Without doubt the cleverest response to the

episode was a poem written by Sarfraz Manzoor in the *Guardian*, which parodied the original poem. It read:

You crossed the oceans in Empire days
Invading nations, imposing British ways
In exchange for cricket you robbed and
*   looted*
Redrew map as you suited
You spoke in English not the native tongue
To old England you passionately clung
And when, finally, we demanded to be free
You invited us here to work in this country
On buses and in factories
In curry houses and as GPs
We worked til late for hard-earned money
Endured racist jokes we didn't find funny
Kept afloat on perspiration
Family values and a faith in education
You were in the pub as we worked all hours
Still you say this land ain't ours
Fit in, you tell us, it's so easy
Just don't ever think you'll be a Tory MP.
Teenage mums and the Asbo generation
We're not the product of immigration

You dump into homes your mum and dad
And blame us for turning Britain bad?
You say we're spongers off the welfare state
But, my friends, it was us who helped
   make Britain great.

The Conservative Party eventually suspended Bland. A spokesman said, 'The Conservative Party disassociates itself entirely from the sentiments in this poem. Ellenor Bland has been suspended from the candidates' list and from the party pending a full investigation.'

It transpired that the poem had also been posted on the forum on Boris Johnson MP's website. Johnson ordered the poem be immediately removed and said, 'It is an utterly dreadful poem and I condemn it unreservedly. Hundreds of people post material on the site and I had absolutely no idea it was there.' One of Johnson's staff confirmed that steps were being taken to ensure that it would become harder for people to post such material on the website in the future.

And Ellenor? At the time of writing, there was no public word on the result of the investigation.

I didn't enter a beauty contest when I became an MP!!!

In the immediate aftermath of the Ellenor Bland scandal, Tory MP Bob Spink managed to create further controversy for the party. During 2006, the MP for Castle Point got involved in an email exchange with a constituent. During the correspondence, the constituent asked, 'Are you saying that a lot more criminals are black than white – or that there are more black people in jail than white because they are stopped more often?'

Spink responded, 'The former and that's what people don't seem to like. But I didn't enter a beauty contest when I became an MP!!!!'

This correspondence was then leaked to the *Daily Mirror*. As a storm erupted around his comments, Spink said that the way his views were being portrayed was 'disingenuous' and 'politically mischievous'.

He added, 'In fact, I was simply repeating to my constituent the answers that the home secretary had put down to me in the House of Commons. I asked a range of questions of the home secretary to establish the facts about crime. He told the House of Commons that, pro rata, many more young black men are known to the criminal justice system than young white men. That is simply a statistical fact.'

He also went onto BBC Radio 4's *Today* programme and said that he wanted to have a 'serious debate' about the issue without 'silly charges of racism being thrown around'. He added, 'It's an MP's duty to be honest and truthful, to set out the facts as they are and to seek to resolve serious problems like where crime is coming from and why there are five times more young black men in prison than young white men.'

Mirror columnist Kevin Maguire wrote, 'Bob Spink. Loathe or detest him, the Essex Foghorn is the authentic nasty face of the Tories as he plays the race card with a relish that turns the stomach.'

A tight rein will be necessary

There's nothing like a good bitch, but it's always best to not conduct such sessions by email. This is a general rule that applies to us all. But, if your conversation is with the man who wants to one day be prime minister, then it is even more imperative that you are discreet.

Conservative leader David Cameron and his parliamentary private secretary Desmond Swayne probably exchange many emails every week. In July 2006, something went badly wrong and a series of emails from Swayne to Cameron found their way to the newspapers.

Much of the content of the emails was relatively innocent. Writing of Francis Maude, Swayne wrote, 'Francis may be a likeable fellow but he is not yet trusted.' Similarly, of Theresa May, he said, 'Theresa is neither liked nor trusted across the party. A tight rein will be necessary.'

He then gives Cameron a few tips: 'My own concern is that you might, if you keep your foot quite so hard on the accelerator, be in danger of being completely frazzled... Lots of unease about political funding and policy "on the hoof" by my estimate is that this is manageable.' Then he advises the leader: 'To keep colleagues content, you must improve your productivity by signing more whisky bottles. We have run out.'

Swayne then warns his leader that Edward Leigh, chair of the influential Commons Public Accounts Committee, wants a meeting with Cameron 'to tell you to your face that you are the Antichrist'. Blimey!

If that wasn't bizarre enough, Swayne then positively teases Cameron – and, thanks to the leak, the rest of the world – when he writes, 'Something dreadful happened to me in Manchester but I cannot put pen to paper. I will tell you later.' No! *Please* tell us now!

The emails came to the attention of the media when printouts of them were found in a Starbucks coffee shop. Another bad day at the office for Cameron, who looks set to rival Blair in the email embarrassment stakes.

Marketing Michael

Michael Simmonds was once the head of marketing and membership for the Conservative Party. He isn't any more. Back in 1999, the Conservative Party was still reeling from the battering it had received from New Labour at the polls two years earlier. This was a bitter blow for a party who had previously won three elections on the trot. Many were predicting that the party was about to become extinct. What was needed was someone with a clear head and real vision.

Instead, they got Michael Simmonds. In 1999, Peter Lilley, then deputy leader of the Conservatives, wrote a speech that outlined plans for the party to break with its Thatcherite past. Simmonds decided to leak it and did so via email. Big mistake. When news broke that the speech had been leaked, the Conservative Party sent a crack team of IT experts to scour the computers of staff at Conservative Central Office. They found Simmonds's email in his 'sent items' box and he was fired.

Just a thought

In 2004, John Stonborough, the press secretary to the Speaker of the House of Commons, Michael Martin, made his own spectacular cyber slip-up. As part of his job, Stonborough had to be an utterly impartial figure. However, when it was revealed that MPs were claiming expenses totalling £78 million, he was enraged. He decided to email the Conservative media chief Guy Black.

The email read: 'Surely, surely the Tories can make something of it? Most of the abuse was Labour. Why not an edict from [party leader Michael] Howard saying you won't overclaim ACA [additional costs allowance], abuse postage for canvassing etc? Puts you back on the sleaze high ground at last and rubbishes the other snouts in trough. Don't wait for the Liberals to do it. Just a thought. Be nice to see you. John S.'

For a supposedly impartial political figure to take sides in this way was exceptionally risky. However, to accidentally send his email not to Guy Black but to another Mr Black who was a Labour researcher was catastrophically stupid.

In a statement, Stonborough said, 'The email was an error of judgement and I resigned from the House of Commons immediately. End of story.'

End of story, indeed. But what a lovely story it was!

CHAPTER FOUR

SEX AND ROMANCE
(PART ONE)

Joseph Dobbie was once a very ordinary man. He was born in Matlock, Derbyshire, and then moved to Slough in Berkshire. He left school at 16 and had spells working as an estate agent and a postman. He then started his own website company, though he found it hard to get clients. Then, one Saturday night he went to a barbecue party and his life changed forever.

This is the part where
I throw caution to the wind

After the barbecue party, Joseph Dobbie became

globally known. He received endless unsolicited phone calls from strangers around the world. Some of these were nice but many more were nasty. In the end, he had to change his phone number.

He was mentioned in Parliament. He was the subject of an in-depth interview profile in the *Daily Mail*. He featured in the opinion pages of national newspapers. The letters page of a newspaper in Sweden was full of praise for him. 'I love Joe Dobbie' T-shirts appeared on eBay, the internet auction site. The US television channel NBC invited him to New York to take part in a chat show.

What had happened at the barbecue party? Had Dobbie discovered a cure for cancer? Had he brokered a solution to the conflicts in the Middle East? No, he had met a woman called Kate Winsall there and was very taken by her as she offered him first some strawberry sponge cake and then some chocolate cake. He asked her if she fancied coming to meet him in Slough one day – wow, make a girl feel special, why don't you? – and found her response ambiguous and flirty.

Then, two days later, he sat down, switched his computer on and opened a new window on his email program. Three hours later, after much soul-searching and rewriting, he had completed the email. He sent it to Kate.

The email read: 'Hello Kate, It's Joe – we met at Andrew's party. I hope you don't mind me getting your e-mail address from the e-mail that Andy sent to us all; it is a bit sneaky of me.

'It was wonderful to meet you on Saturday, and I wonder if you would consider meeting me for coffee sometime; maybe at the Tate Modern? OK. This is where my common sense is telling me to stop. Keep it simple and positive Joe.

'And the probability of me listening to that voice? Experience has taught me that it is not worth putting up a fight; I will end up giving in to the part of me that never wants to find itself shaking its head and muttering "if only?"'

'This is the part where I throw caution to the wind; the part where I listen to my heart and remember that I should live my life as an exultation and revel in the opportunity to try; the part where I refuse to apologise for who I am; the part where I trust that the lady I met on Saturday night is, as I suspect, able to see sincerity where others would see cliche.'

'I am fortunate enough to have been able to collect a number of special memories. They are memories of moments that made any struggle leading up to them worthwhile. They are memories of moments when I am struck by something so beautiful, time stands still and all of the ugliness in the world ceases to exist.

'Your smile is the freshest of my special memories. Regardless of whether we see each other again, I will use it as I do my other special memories. I will call on it when I am disheartened or low. I will hold it in my heart when I need inspiration. I will keep it with me for moments when I need to find a smile of my own.

'I am unsure of all my motives for sharing this with you and, if I am honest, not ready to examine them too closely. However, I know that it makes me feel good to believe that maybe, if you are ever upset, knowing that I will be keeping your smile alive might help you through.

'If you are half as intelligent and aware as I believe you to be, I am sure that you will find

what I have written, in the very least, swe
am twice as lucky as I would dare to hope,
will find this note charming and agree to contact
me and arrange a date.

'Either way, I trust that your reply will be
candid – you told me how much you value
honesty. One last thing, I promise that it is
enormously rare for me to stray as far from
sobriety as I managed on Saturday night. Be
safe. Joe.'

It's OK – it's over now. I promise. You can
uncurl your toes and look out from behind your
fingers. This was ghastly and cringeworthy by
any standards. There truly aren't enough sick
buckets in the world to cope with the natural
reaction any sane person would have if they
received such an email from anyone –
particularly from someone they had only ever
passed a few slices of cake to.

So what was Kate's reaction to receiving this
extraordinary email from the man from
Slough with the name of a movie elf to whom
she once offered some cake? She forwarded
the email to her sister Jane who then
forwarded it on to all her friends with the new

ow to ask a girl out (in a

)' and the additional comment

touch-paper had been lit and

it to begin.

later, Dobbie answered the phone and was told by a friend that his email had been circulated around the world and that he was being laughed at across the globe. The email had found its way on to an American website called The Drudge Report and, soon, over 60,000 people around the world were reading his soppy email and laughing their heads off at him.

The press were quick to pick up on this story and didn't spare his blushes. GLOBAL RIDICULE OVER MAN'S SOPPY EMAIL screamed the *Evening Standard*; THE WORLD CRINGES AT SOPPY JOE'S LOVE NOTE mocked the *Daily Mail*.

Having been thrown into the public eye, Dobbie was not one to hide away and wait for the fuss to blow over. He spoke to many journalists, telling one that he was not at all embarrassed by his email and that he had always been a 'hopeless romantic'. He added that he once sent a girlfriend a Valentine's Day card of wooden hearts he had made by hand from lollipop sticks. He told another that he was writing a book on philosophy based on the idea that world peace is inevitable, with crocodiles a significant factor in this inevitability.

The *Daily Mail* sent a female journalist on a date with Dobbie to see what he was really like in person. The pair met – appropriately enough – at the Tate Modern and Dobbie arrived two minutes early. 'I can see why Kate didn't jump on him. He isn't beautiful,' wrote the journalist. 'He resembles a cross between a malfunctioning robot and a stray dog.'

He insisted he was not angry with Kate at all and felt 'some understanding' for her sister. He outlined the many phone-calls from strangers he had received – he unwisely included his phone number on the email – including one from a group of women who called him on speaker-phone from South Africa and were, he recalls, largely complimentary. He read her a poem he had written that included the lines: 'Staring at the sun and thinking of the moon; wishing it were winter in the middle of June; starting to get thirsty as the bottle runs dry; now I'm coming down although I want to get high.'

Lovely, isn't it? As much of the world wet their pants laughing at him, poor old Dobbie received support from some people. Rebecca Steal wrote on the *Observer* website that she felt sorry for him. She even confessed that, as one of the early recipients of the email, she might have been unwittingly responsible for the email receiving such widespread publicity in the media.

'I sort of feel bad,' she wrote. 'But, even though I've seen his picture in the papers, it's like he doesn't exist, which encapsulates the alarming beauty of the internet: when you've pinged that email off into cyberspace and deleted it from the sent box, you can easily delude yourself into thinking it's vanished into the ether, never to be read.'

She threw down the gauntlet to her readers and invited them to use the Comment function on the article's webpage to give messages of support to Dobbie. One reader, with the username 'marcavaro' stepped up to the task.

'Marcavaro' wrote, 'We should all big up Joe Dobbie I suppose. Poor guy. It reminds me why I left the UK. Poetry died years ago and it is considered unacceptable to say anything mildly romantic to a girl. Damn cold, miserable, unfriendly, embittered and inarticulate sceptred isles. I shall avoid returning for some time.'

It is my utter mission to track down this dude

Joseph Dobbie clearly should have played it a bit more cool – but then the same can be said for Vicky Elborough-Cook. Following a row with her boyfriend, the 24-year-old from Broxbourne in Hertfordshire went to Barcelona on a hen weekend. There she met a man called Gavin Monks, a BBC employee who was in Spain for a stag weekend. The pair flirted with one another but, when Monks asked her for her phone number, she declined to give it to him.

However, once she got home, she bitterly regretted being so coy and decided to try and track down Monks. She sent an email around various contacts and friends, asking if they could help put her in touch with Monks.

The email read: 'Hi... I was in Barcelona between 14–16 July and met a guy called GAVIN from KENT who was on a stag weekend... staying at Hotel Auto Hogar (never go there it's rubbish!)

'Gavin said he writes the "i" for the BBC... (when you press 'i' on digital a brief synopsis of the programme is shown etc...)

'Now...thru playing hard to get... i didn't give him my phone number! :(... tho he did ask several times.

'Please can you let me known where an "i" writer would work!! It is my utter mission to track down this dude... he is utterly gorgeous and i was an idiot for acting so damn stooped!

'Sorry for my randomness... but PLEASE help! Thanks, Vicky x'

Well, to say that Elborough-Cook was through with playing hard to get was an under-statement. Her email was quickly circulated to terminals around the globe and, before long, thousands were having a good laugh at the former convent schoolgirl's 'utter mission' to track down 'this dude'. BBC offices around the world received countless copies of the email.

The twist in the tale lies in the fact that, between her first sending the email and it becoming globally known, Monks had actually got in touch with her. Having got her phone number from one of her friends, he had made contact with Elborough-Cook and the two had struck up a friendly and promising rapport.

However, once Monks heard about her email and how it was snowballing around the world, he texted her asking, 'Why are you stalking me?' The relationship was over before it had even got started.

'"God, get over yourself",' she says. 'If he didn't find that email at all cute, he's not for me. He turned out to be a bit of a loser.'

She decided to try and rebuild her relationship with her boyfriend, a pharmacological neuroscientist. 'I think he's managing to see the funny side of it all,' she said. However, she admitted that her parents would struggle to find any humour in the episode. 'My mum will shoot me over this,' she predicted.

We started having sex. I noticed his eyes were closed for a little too long

One day, Manhattan resident Trip Murray sent an email to his new lover Mary B Callahan. It was innocuous stuff: he asked if she was going to see Bon Jovi play at Madison Square Garden and mentioned a party that he was planning to attend. Having read the email, Callahan intended to forward it to a friend with a note of her own attached. However, rather than hit 'forward', she hit 'reply'. When you read what her note was, you will see what an awful error this was.

It read: 'OK first-here is the e-mail I received from Trip, the new guy I met last week. If you want to go out, perhaps we can get him to pay for drinks at Park. Since we have not slept together, he will of course be trying to impress me and will, therefore, do anything I ask. Unlike John, who fell asleep during sex last night. I went over to his place last night around 11:30. We started having sex. When I noticed his eyes were closed for a little too long, I said, "John, wake up." At which point, he shot up saying "what'd I miss?" Yes, I think that is a new low.

'Let me know about tonight. I think you need company.'

When Murray received the email, he instantly forwarded it to a friend of his. 'Please, read my email first. Then read her email, I think that she was forwarding my email to a friend but hit reply instead. You will love this.'

He must have loved it because he then

forwarded it to a friend and, before long, people around the world were loving it. As it whizzed around the world, the usual commentary got attached by gleeful recipients. 'Drop what you're doing and read this. The following is an exchange between a friend of a guy that sits on our desk and a girl he took out on a date. Read from the bottom up. Oh my lord.'

Another forwarder said, 'How long will it take for this one to go around and around! Read below. TREMENDOUS!'

I am totally faithful, extremely sincere and passionate

After Mark Ridgewell divorced from his wife Alison, he wanted to find a new love. So the father of two registered with the udate.com website – called 'little more than a cyber meat market' by one newspaper – and posted up a profile. On it he described himself as a 6ft 2in management consultant earning up to £75,000 per year. He said he played rugby and read the *Financial Times*. He also said he was 'caring and extremely reliable'.

Once he got chatting with women on the

website, he called them 'Princess' and 'Sexy' and told them that he was 'totally faithful, extremely sincere and passionate'. He sent romantic late-night texts and Daniel Bedingfield CDs to potential dates. He even mailed them musical emails with MP3s of songs like Stevie Wonder's 'You Are The Sunshine Of My Life' attached. However, 44-year-old Ridgewell was not as caring or faithful as he made out.

One of the women he met through the dating website was artist Dawn Knight. The 37-year-old remembers first becoming suspicious of Ridgewell when, while she was at his home in the Cotswolds, his doorbell and mobile phone both rang but he said that it was related to work.

A few days later, though, Ridgewell really dropped himself in it. He had been juggling dates with at least four different women at the same time without any of them knowing he was seeing anyone else. So, when he sent a saucy email to Knight and accidentally copied it to three of the other women he was seeing, he really was in trouble. The women contacted one another and set up a glorious sting.

Knight invited Ridgewell for a drink at his favourite pub, The Wheatsheaf in Gloucester. They bought a drink and, as Ridgewell relaxed with his pint of Guinness, Knight sent a signal via mobile phone to the other women. When he found himself confronted by all four women, Ridgewell's face was a treat, as readers of the *Gloucestershire Echo* will know – the women had invited along a photographer to capture the moment on film. The scorned women fired questions at Ridgewell and all he could splutter in return was 'No comment.'

One of the women told reporters that she was more angry following the confrontation than she had been beforehand. 'I wanted to punch his lights out,' she spat.

Another stormed, 'It's not even as if he's good-looking. I hope he rots in hell.'

In the aftermath of the sting, Ridgewell combined sheepish denials with cocky boasts. At first, he accused the women of being mistaken. He said that most of them were simply friends and if they thought he was dating them all then they were mistaken. He then called them 'bunny boilers' and compared himself to

Michael Douglas's character in *Fatal Attraction*.

He also said that he hoped that Guinness would see that when he was busted he was drinking their stout and would consequently invite him to advertise the drink under the slogan of 'Guinness, the drink of stallions'. Later he said it was lucky that only four women turned up to the sting as it could have been 'many, many more'.

The press loved the whole affair and how the 'serial seducer was snared in a love trap'. One newspaper headline jeered to Ridgewell that he was IN FOUR IT.

Before long, he had also registered with the Friends Reunited website. On his profile there, the man who was known as Ridgy and Wingnut at the Friary Grange secondary school, said he was 'divorced with kids' and added 'you would have thought I would have learned!' Quickly, a tabloid journalist posing as a fellow former pupil was in contact and flirting online with him, before repeating the correspondence in the newspaper.

During the exchange, she told him that she was impressed by the stories of his infidelity. 'At last somebody from Friary has got a bit of fame!'

In one of his messages, he wrote of his regret that she could not meet up with him that week. 'What a shame! It's a real shame – with what's been going on this week it would have been lovely to have a chill and a chat! And boy after this week I need a chat about all that's been going on!'

Such people are a tabloid newspaper journalist's dream come true.

There was further fallout from the affair when one of the women involved with the pub sting was given a month's sick leave from work. Janet Graham, who worked for Morgan Stanley International Banking Corporation, was said to have been deeply affected by the ordeal.

You are disgusting. Please leave.

It's not known if colleagues of Janice Kostelnik said, 'What a lovely bird! Just bootiful!' when they received suggestive nude pictures of her via email one morning, but, given that they worked at the head office of turkey tycoon Bernard Matthews, it is nice to think they did.

The photos were emailed to Janice and to six of her colleagues after she walked out on her husband Karl. An unemployed training consultant from Norfolk, Karl took their split very badly and emailed 11 saucy photos of his wife to her and her colleagues at their office. For good measure, he followed up with an email to Janice, which purported to be sent by one of her colleagues. It read: 'You are disgusting. We don't want to work with you. Please leave.'

Janice was understandably upset by this and fled the office. She then called the police and reported what her estranged husband had done. He was charged with two counts of sending an indecent message containing grossly offensive material.

When he faced trial at Cromer Magistrates, Karl claimed that he meant to only send the photos to his wife but accidentally sent them to the six colleagues when he clicked the 'reply all' button on his screen. He also admitted sending photos deliberately on a subsequent occasion and confessed to sending the 'please leave' message.

The stipendiary magistrate told Karl, 'This behaviour almost beggars belief in its mean-spiritedness and disloyalty.' He handed Karl a two-month suspended prison sentence.

I've got an extremely small penis that couldn't excite a woman's nostril

There cannot be many people who would send an email admitting to being a 'snivelling, arrogant little piece of shit'. And, even though an email starting with just those words was sent from his account, Paul Evans is not one of those people.

The vitriolic email sent from Paul's account was in fact penned by his wife Tracey. She suspected that her husband of seven years had been cheating on her, though there was no proof that her suspicions were correct. The couple lived in Dorset and had two daughters. However, following Tracey's 3am email blast, things would never be the same.

The email – titled 'Time To Fess Up!' – read: 'Dear everyone, Well I guess it's now time to come clean (unheard of for me, I know). OK, here goes. I, Paul Owen Evans, am a snivelling, arrogant little piece of shit.

'No, that's not right – I'm worse than that: I'm a despicable, dirty, DICKHEAD who doesn't reserve this attitude just for his wife. Oh yes, one more thing – I've got an extremely small penis that couldn't excite a woman's nostril, let alone anything else.'

The message was sent to his 50 most important business contacts. Meanwhile, Paul, a PR manager, was in Barcelona overseeing the press launch of a new car. He first heard of the email when a friend contacted him by phone.

The mail was sent to leading figures in the car industry, top rally drivers, contacts and friends of Paul. It also went to people at his firm. However, it was estimated that, within hours of it being sent out, up to 100,000 people might have seen it as it pinged around the world.

Paul tried to prevent it from going further by pleading with bosses at the Volkswagen group to block the emails from coming on to their server. However, his request was made too late as the message was already being read by workers in the company.

Meanwhile, the couple's Dorset home was besieged by reporters. Tracey initially refused to go into details of she sent out the angry email. She did confirm that it was because she believed her husband had been unfaithful and her electronic missive provided proof that the

email of the species is indeed more deadly than
the male.

James was home, but you've guessed it, he was not alone!

Jim Pritchard is a public relations executive for
car-parking giants NCP, but in December 2006
he encountered a public relations disaster in
his personal life. Pritchard, an amateur
footballer, was born in Nottingham. However,
when his heartbroken girlfriend of two years
decided to show him the red card, she
accidentally did so in front of a Premiership-
sized audience.

When she discovered Pritchard cheating on
her, Tamsin Craigie sent an email to a handful of
friends and colleagues at Westminster Council.
Craigie sounded off about how hurt she was and
announced she was breaking up with him.

The email began with her recalling how she
had been fooled into thinking their
relationship had just taken a turn for the
better: 'He told me he wasn't contemplating
whether he wanted a relationship with me but
rather more along the lines of marriage and

children. I could not believe my ears! Has the boy grown up all of a sudden?'

She admitted that she hoped 'that everything would be just fine, he would return from work, propose to me, tell me how much he loved me and how sorry he was... but no, none of that.'

Then, after a night out drinking, she turned up at his Balham flat. 'Bang, my world shattered into a billion pieces! James was home, but you've guessed it, he was not alone! Instead, he was with some poor young blonde girl who had obviously fallen for his charm!

'I am the third poor foolish girl that he has cheated on – the man's a selfish, pathetic bastard' and a 'useless pile of shit' but she had 'eventually come to her senses'.

She concluded, 'So that is it. Mr Pritchard is officially dumped and if I ever see him again it will be too soon!'

However, although she only sent this email to 24 friends and workmates, and without any proof that Jim had been up to no good, at least one of the recipients forwarded it on to a friend and it soon pinged around the world and into the newspapers. Newspaper reporters were soon chasing the couple and besieging their employers with questions. Westminster Council would only say it was 'a private matter', while NCP said, 'It's not exactly Madonna and Guy Ritchie we are talking about.'

Craigie had initially only sent the email as 'a psychological step' and to save her 'the embarrassment of tears at work'. You can only imagine how much the huge subsequent embarrassment affected her psychologically.

'Love, Todd.'

Marketing man Todd Andrlik finished off an email to his wife one day and signed it 'Love, Todd.' Seems reasonable, doesn't it? However, he then returned to work duties and fired off an email to a journalist contact, trying to sell a product to her. With the sign-off from his previous email still in his mind, Andrlik signed off this email 'Love, Todd' too.

He realised his error the moment he clicked 'send'. 'Fortunately, I knew the reporter and immediately called her to clarify that, while I do enjoy her stories and value her relationship, our working bond hadn't escalated to "love" just yet,' he explained on his blog. 'I briefly explained the circumstances and the reporter laughed it off. She wrote the story too.'

I wish I had never set eyes on the guy in the first place

A story I received during my research for this book puts Andrlik's story well and truly in the shade. A woman in her twenties emailed me to tell me how email humiliated her in front of her family.

She wrote, 'I had swapped mobile numbers with a guy from my local gym a few days before this happened. We had been exchanging texts a lot and some of them were quite detailed about what we like getting up to in the sack.

'He sent me his email address by text and suggested we carried on our conversation there. I ended up getting quite carried away and writing a particularly horny email to him. Let's just say it covered nearly every sexual fantasy I have ever had.

'The thing is, I accidentally emailed it to my aunt. She has the same first letter as the guy from the gym and so as soon as I typed that letter into the 'To' field, it automatically brought up my aunt's email address. Before I knew what was happening, I had sent the email off. I've never been more shocked in my life.

'After one of the most horrible and traumatic 24 hours of my life, I wrote her a second email, asking that she just delete and try to forget the email. I told her it was only a joke. She replied and said, "What email? I've forgotten already."

'However, the following Christmas when the family got together, I got the distinct feeling that more family members than just my aunt had been made aware of my email. I could just tell by the way they all went quiet when I walked into the room. Even more disturbingly, my uncle seemed to be more friendly to me than ever.

'In the end, I never did hook up with the guy from the gym. The whole thing had upset me so much, I just wanted to forget about all of it. To be honest, I wish I had never set eyes on the guy in the first place.'

CHAPTER FIVE

MEDIA FOLK

'Have you ever messed up with email? Has sending the wrong email to the wrong person ever destroyed your life, held you up to enormous ridicule and left you in emotional tatters? Has email lost you your job, your home, your partner and your dignity? Then give us a ring.' Were Robert Kilroy-Silk to present a show on great email disasters, that is how he might well research it. And, were he to host such a show, he could draw on personal experience, because the orange-faced, grey-haired former MP once fell victim to a great email disaster of his own.

Oh, you like shit, do you?
Let me give it to you back.

In 2004, the *Sunday Express* printed a column by Kilroy-Silk under the headline WE OWE ARABS NOTHING. It began, 'We are told by some of the more hysterical critics of the war on terror that it is destroying the Arab world. So? Should we be worried about that? Shouldn't the destruction of the despotic, barbarous and corrupt Arab states and their replacement by democratic governments be a war aim?'

Hmm, just what the world needed at such a tense time. But the most controversial passage in the column read: 'What do they think we feel about them? That we adore them for the way they murdered more than 3,000 civilians on September 11 and then danced in the hot, dusty streets to celebrate the murders?

'That we admire them for the cold-blooded killings in Mombasa, Yemen and elsewhere? That we admire them for being suicide bombers, limb-amputators, women repressors? I don't think the Arab states should start a debate about what is really loathsome.'

Not surprisingly, Kilroy-Silk's column quickly provoked an unholy row – one that involved everyone from *Sunday Express* sub-editors to race-relations groups, the BBC, the House of Commons, the Hutton Report and the police. The story involves numerous accusations and counter-accusations. However, it turned out that a simple email error was responsible for sparking the controversy.

Kilroy-Silk was topping up his famous tan in Spain when, back in the UK, his secretary Hilary Hunter emailed his column to the *Sunday Express*, as she did every week. It was a particularly busy and hectic day for Hunter, with new staff starting work at her office. Instead of sending the correct column – which raged about foreigners getting free treatment on the NHS – she emailed a column that the newspaper had already published the previous year.

Unfortunately, the editorial team at the *Sunday Express* didn't notice they had been sent a column they had already published, so they published it again in that weekend's newspaper. However, when the column had been run the previous year, sub-editors at the *Sunday*

Express had made a small but crucial alteration. They changed the focus of Kilroy-Silk's 'suicide bombers, limb-amputators and women repressors' accusation to 'Arab countries', rather than simply 'Arabs'.

That alteration had helped to ensure that the first airing of his column passed without controversy. However, when the column was run for a second time as a result of Hunter's email error, this toning down was not repeated and the column therefore made this accusation against Arab people in general.

Cue widespread outrage, with Commission for Racial Equality chairman Trevor Phillips the first out of the traps. 'The article was indisputably stupid,' he raged. 'It trivialised one of the most important and difficult areas of international relations facing the world today.'

He went on, 'Given the extreme and violent terms in which Mr Kilroy-Silk has expressed himself, there is a danger that this might incite some individuals to act against someone who they think is an Arab.

'Our lawyers have considered the column and, in the light of widespread concern, we are referring the article to the police to consider whether it might constitute an offence under the Public Order Act.'

Sunday Express editor Martin Townsend was quick to attempt to wash his hands of the matter. He said, 'I must stress that the views expressed in Robert's column are not those of the newspaper.' Meanwhile, another source at the newspaper insisted that the mood among the team there was 'upbeat and very determined'.

The newspaper and Kilroy-Silk then had a bit of a squabble about how the Arabs/Arab countries variation came about. In the orange corner, Kilroy-Silk insisted that his original column referred to 'Arab countries' and that this was changed by the *Sunday Express* to 'Arabs' for the second airing. However, the newspaper insisted that his original column referred to 'Arabs' and that this was changed first-time round to 'Arab countries' by a sub-editor and that this change had not been made for the most recent publication.

In his column the following weekend, Kilroy-Silk also pointed the finger at his secretary. 'Last week I wrote my column as usual – about John

Reid's proposal to charge foreigners for using the NHS at it happens. It did not appear. Instead, the article I had written the previous April was reprinted. This was a mistake. My secretary apparently clicked on the wrong email attachment and dispatched the old one.'

Hunter admitted that the error was down to her and said she was wearing 'sackcloth and ashes'. She also revealed the slightly tortuous process that publication of her boss's column went through. 'He doesn't know how to type or about emails or how to file them,' she said. 'He writes them in longhand, faxes them to me, I type them out, fax them back, we correct any mistakes then I email them to the *Sunday Express* features editor.'

She accused those who had complained about the article of doing so to stir up trouble. 'Robert is very fair-minded,' she said. 'He is not racist at all – he employs a black driver.' Wow, you can't get much more fair-minded than that!

As well as blaming Hunter, Kilroy-Silk fair-mindedly pointed the finger at the BBC and the 'forces of political correctness'. He also referred to the Second World War and how his father had 'died defending the rights to freedom'.

More was to follow. In the wake of the Hutton Report, the BBC had banned some of its star names from writing newspaper columns. John Humphrys and John Simpson were among those who had been forced to drop the lucrative side-incomes they received from Fleet Street. The Arab Media Watch group was quick to point out that Kilroy-Silk was potentially contradicting the post-Hutton guidelines by writing his *Sunday Express* column.

This was of course a perfect story for the press, including as it did a mainstream, daytime television presenter, allegations of racism and the possibility of a triple-scalp. Could Kilroy-Silk lose his job at the BBC, his column *and* be convicted of breaking anti-racism laws? They were quick to point out that the latter outcome could see him jailed for seven years.

The BBC confirmed that it was investigating the incident, including the question of whether his column contravened the Hutton guidelines. As for the *Sunday Express*, they offered the Muslim Council of Britain the chance to write an article in response to Kilroy-Silk's column. Even then, they managed to offend the group when they insisted that the rebuttal article could not include the offensive terms included in the original column. The paper eventually backed down and ran the Muslim Council's article complete with the original terms.

With all sides now blaming each other for the controversy, the whole affair was shaping up to be as entertaining as the barneys that sometimes broke out on BBC1's *Kilroy*, whose presenter could only have dreamed of such drama and fury taking place in the studio. Thanks in part to the popularity of his show, Kilroy-Silk received huge support from the public during the row. Ninety-seven per cent of *Sunday Express* readers said the BBC was wrong to suspend him and 93 per cent of Sky television viewers agreed in a separate poll. Thousands of callers complained to the BBC about the suspension.

Kilroy-Silk was much cheered by this show of support and said it was reflected by his own experiences when he visited the theatre and people came up to him to pledge their support.

He was also backed by a 62-year-old nurse from Kidderminster called Mary O'Nions who had been tortured and caged in Saudi Arabia. She had also witnessed brutal floggings of other women in the jail. 'He is speaking what a lot of people think but dare not say,' she said of the beleaguered columnist.

Kilroy-Silk also received the backing of Ibrahim Nawar, the head of Arab Press Freedom Watch. Nawar said, 'I fully support Robert Kilroy-Silk and salute him as an advocate of freedom of expression. I would like to voice my solidarity with him and with all those who face the censorship of such a basic human right. I agree with much of what he says about Arab regimes. There is a very long history of oppression in the Arab world, particularly in the states he mentions: Iran, Iraq, Algeria, Egypt, Libya, Yemen, Saudi Arabia, as well as in Sudan and Tunisia.'

However, despite this support, the BBC decided to axe the *Kilroy* programme and the presenter was forced to quit after bosses were believed to have told him to resign or face the chop. Kilroy-Silk was defiant: 'I continue to believe it is my right to express my views, however uncomfortable they may be. However, I recognise the difficulties this has caused the BBC.'

His torment was not over, however. In December 2004, as he prepared to appear as a guest on BBC Radio 4's *Any Questions*, Kilroy-Silk was attacked by an unemployed man from Cheshire. David McGrath threw a bucket of farmyard manure over Kilroy-Silk. 'You insulted my brother's religion. You insulted Islam,' shouted McGrath as he covered the presenter in poo.

Kilroy-Silk later described how, 'out of a sense of outrage and disgust', he then wiped some of the manure from his suit and smeared it over McGrath's face, saying, 'Oh, you like shit, do you? Let me give it to you back.' I wish I'd been there.

McGrath's attack had also resulted in the new education minister Ruth Kelly and Kilroy-Silk's driver both getting splattered with manure. McGrath, 37, later pleaded guilty in court to three counts of causing criminal damage and one public order offence. However, he was given a conditional discharge and walked free from court.

In a legal document that was read out in

court, Kilroy-Silk said, 'As a result of an unprovoked attack, I am now very apprehensive about future public appearances and worried about my personal safety. I dread to think what the consequences could have been if the person had been in possession of a knife or other lethal weapon.

'My wife and daughter have been extremely upset about the incident and my wife is considering "risk assessment" to reduce the risk of future incidents occurring.'

Making sure your secretary takes more care over sending out emails might be a start, Robert!

Now fuck off and cover something important you twats!

Spin doctor Alastair Campbell says that throughout his Downing Street years he was a self-confessed technophobe who went nowhere near email. He wrote, 'I was blessed in Downing Street with a wonderful team of assistants who would *inter alia* sift emails sent to me, show me the ones they thought I needed to see, and then type up my handwritten replies to those I thought I needed to give a response. I know, I know, it sounds implausible, pathetic even. But it worked for me.'

However, once he left Downing Street, the marathon-running, foul-mouthed Campbell quickly converted to the joys of cyberspace. He bought a Blackberry and admits to quickly becoming 'addicted to the little toy on my belt'. Then, in February 2005, he made his first email slip-up. BBC 2's *Newsnight* programme began probing Campbell's role in the controversial posters that Labour used during the 2005 general election campaign. The posters had depicted the Conservatives' Jewish leader Michael Howard as Fagin, which prompted complaints that the posters were anti-Semitic.

Newsnight was investigating claims that Labour's advertising agency TBWA was blaming Campbell for the posters. Campbell quickly fired off an email from his Blackberry suggesting that Labour HQ get TBWA boss Trevor Beattie to issue a statement clearing this up. The email was intended for an official at Labour HQ but Campbell accidentally sent it to *Newsnight* journalist Andrew McFadyen.

The email read: 'Just spoke to Trev. Think

TBWA shd give statement to *Newsnight* saying party and agency work together well and nobody here has spoken to standard. Posters done by TBWA according to political brief. Now fuck off and cover something important you twats!'

On checking his 'sent items' box, Campbell discovered – doubtless with a few choice words – his mistake. So he quickly fired off a second message to McFadyen.

This time, he wrote, 'Not very good at this e-mail Blackberry malarkey. Just looked at log of sent messages, have realised email meant for colleagues at TBWA has gone to you. For the record, first three sentences of email spot on. No row between me and Trevor.

'Posters done by them according to our brief. I dreamt up flying pigs. Pigs not great but OK in the circs of Tories promising tax cuts and spending rises with the same money. TBWA made production.

'Campbell swears shock. Final sentence of earlier email probably a bit colourful and personal considering we have never actually met but I'm sure you share the same sense of humour as your star presenter Mr P. [Jeremy Paxman].

'Never known such a silly fuss since the last silly fuss but there we go. Must look forward not back.'

A source from *Newsnight* confirmed that on receiving the email they concluded that Campbell had 'gone bonkers'. Meanwhile, Campbell's former deputy Tim Allan said, 'Judging by his email, it is time to disengage the Blackberry and re-engage the brain.'

The press, many of whom Campbell had berated and shouted at down the years, were quick to sling mud at him. A leading article in the *Independent* newspaper mourned 'the unwelcome reappearance of Alastair Campbell' and accused him of being an unprofessional bully. It said of his ranting message to *Newsnight*: '[It] could be dismissed if it came from a foul-mouthed viewer but, when it comes from a figure who is, once again, at the heart of our government, the media must take it seriously.'

There was not much more support for him from his successor, who simply shrugged that Campbell was 'capable of speaking for himself'.

A month after his Blackberry episode, Campbell hit the headlines as a result of another modern-day technology incident. It was alleged that he had been sending amorous text messages to the attractive TV newsreader Katie Derham, after having met her at a party and hit it off with her. However, the happily married Derham was quick to deny that the texts were anything other than work-related.

She said, 'I have received text messages, but they were only work messages. A lot more has been made of these texts than there really is. Alastair has a good relationship with lots of journalists. We get on well, but to suggest anything more is very out of order.'

If you're sensitive about a weight issue, you shouldn't be in a job that's so high profile

Agnes Wilkie, the head of features and entertainment at Scottish Television, knew a thing or two about dramas before she fell victim to a great email disaster. She was behind a string of successful shows including _Scottish Passport_, _Scottish Women_, _The Home Show_ and the gritty council-block soap opera _High Times_, which won awards including a Scottish Bafta.

Wilkie was known as 'the Rottweiler' because

of her no-nonsense style of work. It is not known whether she approved of her nickname or found it offensive, but her description of another member of staff at Scottish Television was about to get 'the Rottweiler' into a lot of trouble.

In an email to one of her colleagues, Wilkie called the company's managing director Bobby Hain 'a fat thing'. Somehow, this email found its way to her boss and she was suspended on full pay and marched out of the building by security guards.

Hain had only joined the company the previous year, having worked in radio at stations including Beat 106, Virgin Radio and Northsound. Wilkie, however, had worked for the company for 24 years and her colleagues were shocked to see her escorted out as a result of her email. 'Everyone in the building has been stunned by this overreaction. It really is a case of using a sledgehammer to crack a nut.'

It was alleged that Wilkie's email had gone further than just referring to Hain as a 'fat thing'. Management at Scottish Television claimed it also compared him to television character Mr Blobby, with references to 'blobby' and 'blobbiness'.

Wilkie denied this but it was not enough to save her and she was sacked.

The case hit the headlines and newspapers pointed out that the company had recently scrapped 59 jobs. When television presenters Carol Smillie and Kaye Adams came out in support of Wilkie, it was suggested that money-saving may have been a factor behind her sacking.

Smillie said, 'It's schoolyard stuff, really. A very trivial remark has been used to mask a bigger problem. If you're sensitive about a weight issue, you shouldn't be in a job that's so high profile. You've got to roll with the punches. God knows, we onscreen people don't take it personally and the critics say horrible things about us all the time.'

Adams added, 'It's sad for everybody. Bobby Hain is hurt. Agnes is massively humiliated. What's gained in the end? Saving money, is that what it's all about?'

Despite outrage at its reaction to the email, Scottish TV insisted it had acted fairly. A spokesperson said, 'Scottish TV is a people business and we believe that everyone here deserves to be treated properly and with dignity by their colleagues. We operate sensible email guidelines for all staff ... Where employees act contrary to company policy, the company has a duty to take action.'

Ken Barlow RIP

Since *Coronation Street* was first broadcast on 9 December 1960, it has become a British institution and the pride and joy of ITV. It is Britain's longest-running television soap opera and is consistently the medium's highest ratings-puller.

As chief executive of ITV, Charles Allen had special reason to be proud of *Coronation Street*. He once took Tony Blair for a drink at the Rovers Return pub and was given a cobble from the Street as a souvenir. Given the ratings that Corrie pulls in – it is normally watched by 11 million viewers – you could forgive Allen for being a bit boastful of the show's success.

When a special plotline reaches its climax, the ratings shoot up even higher. This happened when long-term *Corrie* character Mike Baldwin died. It was a dramatic moment as Baldwin –

who had been suffering from Alzheimer's disease – died in the arms of his long-term rival Ken Barlow. This was a huge moment in the show's history, so much so that it inspired *Radio Times* magazine to recreate *The Death Of Nelson* painting, featuring Baldwin in the Admiral's pose, surrounded by fellow members of the *Corrie* cast.

The ratings for this episode climbed from 11 million to 12 million – that's a 58 per cent share of the audience. Allen was enormously excited by this, so much so that he emailed the ITV staff to boast about the huge ratings that the event had attracted. A pity, then, he chose to speak of the death of Ken Barlow.

She is a nightmare to work with. I hate her.

Not that TV folk only mess up by email – they can make utter buffoons of themselves via text messages too! Benedetta Pinelli was a successful producer on the GMTV show when she and Lorraine Kelly went to Africa to record an item in Namibia about Brad Pitt's visit to the country. While there, the pair had a serious disagreement about the work of cameraman Steve Smith – Kelly's husband.

A fuming Pinelli wrote a text message to her husband: 'My God, I have really got the hump, I have just had a massive bust-up with LK. She is a nightmare to work with. I hate her.' Pinelli then sent the message – to Lorraine Kelly's mobile phone!

An ITV source told reporters, 'Lorraine is very sweet-natured and didn't say anything about it, but when they got back to London Benedetta offered her resignation.'

That resignation was accepted and Pinelli now works elsewhere.

I think they're both crap

Anything TV folk can do, radio people can do better. In 1995, BBC sports journalist Graeme Reid-Davies outlined what he thought made for a good sports-commentary style. 'Sure, you've got to do your preparation,' he said. 'But the information you give out must be interesting.' Six years later, he got caught up in an interesting mess himself.

In December 2001, Radio Five Live proudly

unveiled two new signings to cover the 2002 World Cup. Sky Sports' Andy Gray and Jonathan Pearce had both come on board and this represented a major coup for all involved. Reid-Davies, by now an executive editor of BBC Sports News, reacted by sending an email to Gordon Turnbull, head of BBC Radio Sport. 'I think they're both crap,' he wrote. Fair comment, you may say, but Reid-Davies accidentally sent the email not just to Turnbull but to 500 members of the BBC sports staff – including new signings Gray and Pearce!

On discovering what he had done, the horrified Reid-Davies attempted a little damage limitation. 'We all make mistakes – and I just made a big one!' read the subject line of a hastily written follow-up. The email read: 'Apologies – having just had a long chat with Gordon about the good news regarding Andy Gray and Jonathan Pearce, I sent a joke email to him – and the rest of you. Just a private joke with the wrong keyboard key hit – sense of humour and all that. Happy Christmas.'

He said later, 'It was just a joke between two old friends. I would not be doing the job I am doing if

I really thought those things. Everyone's laughing at me. I can't believe I was such an arse.'

I think he should get some professional help, he's clearly insane

Anyone who has seen the hours that television devotes to football analysis knows that players who can talk as well as play a good game are guaranteed plenty of work. Well, get ready, viewers – there might be a new pundit on his way to you!

Mike Rolt, a former public schoolboy in his twenties, plays football for the old boys of Radley College. One day, the manager of the team, James Townley, asked Rolt if he might be willing to change position and play on the right of midfield.

Rolt's emailed reply was simply astonishing. It sounded more like a *Sky Sports* analysis of a Premiership match than a simple message about an old boys team and brought much mockery on the head of Rolt.

In its full pomp, his message read:

I've thought about this quite hard and I just think that it's a waste of our fittest player. I know I'm quick and it would be useful out wide but, unless George Mac or Tim were playing in midfield, I wouldn't be very involved.

Also pace is very effective in the centre as well for intercepting passes/covering tackles/catching them on the break etc. I am also one of the better tacklers and headers of the ball and am also probably the most vocal.

Sticking me out on the wing would lose us these attributes. I wouldn't have much running to do and, although I'll beat my man three or four times, the play will get over-congested down the left or in the middle and I'll end up starved.

In an ideal world, with everybody fit and available, I would play on the right or even up front where I played with some success at Uni. Steven Gerrard has a good role at Liverpool on the right but with the freedom to roam.

That ONLY works, however, because they have Sissoko and Alonso in the middle – two holding midfielders – one of which can spray the ball around.

Unfortunately, we don't have the players for this, although Tommy Hodge and Tim would be fantastic.

Mark and Han in the middle just doesn't work because they aren't positionally aware enough, get caught forward and distribution suffers, the best example of which is Brentwood last season. We sucked.

But what really sucked for Rolt was that the team manager forwarded his email to three people, one of whom forwarded it further. Before long, it was whizzing around the computer terminals of the City faster than Thierry Henry.

Inevitably, as it gained circulation, it attracted comments. One of the recipients wrote, 'Sweet god – this is incredible – I'm surprised he isn't playing in the Prem or maybe England – he sounds amazing.'

Another was more to the point: 'I think he should get some professional help, he's clearly insane.'

Team manager Townley was concerned to hear that the email had been leaked, but he was more bemused by the email itself. 'All I said was you should be playing on the right for the good of the team and I got this small novel,' he sighed.

Kazakhstan Government has serious concerns about the Borat character

Just as the small screen has had its funny email moments, so has the big screen. Most people managed to see that Sacha Baron Cohen's character Borat was intended to be funny. Even Kazakhstan's President Nursultan Nazarbayev got the joke when he said, 'The film was created by a comedian so let's laugh at it, that's my attitude.'

However, as the film *Borat: Cultural Learnings Of America For Make Benefit Glorious Nation Of Kazakhstan* was released, some English diplomats hit the panic button about the film causing offence. In emails between the various officials, over a month was spent discussing how they should respond to the film.

One email read: 'Kazakhstan Government has serious concerns about the Borat character. His site is banned by Kazakhstan tele-communications operator.'

A Foreign Office employee wrote: 'My concern

here is to put us at arm's length from the actor a bit more and for there to be no hint of us defending him, while pointing out, of course, that we have a free media.'

CHAPTER SIX

THE OFFICE
(PART TWO)

'It's my party and I'll cry if I want to,' sang Lesley Gore. Well, Lucy Gao could be forgiven if she shed a few tears over her 21st birthday – after all, people around the world sobbed with laughter when they read her infamous email detailing instructions for her party guests.

It goes without saying that the more upper-class you dress, the less likely you shall be denied entry

Lucy Gao is the daughter of successful parents. She went to Parkstone Grammar School for Girls in Dorset and went on to study engineering at Balliol College, Oxford. After that, she took up an internship with Citigroup in Real Estate Equity Research at the bank's headquarters in Canary Wharf, London. She had the world at her feet.

She also had the world at her fingertips, as she discovered during the week of her 21st birthday party. She emailed around 40 friends who were due to attend her party at London's swish Ritz hotel. Sadly for Gao, one of her 'friends' forwarded the message to a colleague. In a matter of hours, the message had been forwarded around Citigroup, with a growing chain of amused commentary. 'You have to read this from the intern working on the property team – I can hardly contain myself,' said one.

Another said, 'I don't like to spread things. I feel quite bad really – but you just have to read this!'

Indeed, you do. So here is Gao's email in full:

Dear Friends, Thank you for all your replies and I am glad all of you can come this Friday to celebrate my 21st with me. Please read ALL the following to ensure your entry into the Ritz.

☻ THE OFFICE (PART TWO) ☻

Lucy's 21st Birthday Party at The Ritz
Hotel London
Friday, 18th of August
9pm Champagne Reception
10pm Photo Shoots
10:30pm Blowing Candles
Mid-night Pangaea, Mayfair

I have arranged the Ritz to host a Champagne Reception with a selection of Ritz Champagne for all my guests, this will be on me so please come and indulge.

A specially made birthday cake has also been ordered and the Ritz waiters will kindly serve you each a generous slice with Ritz cutleries, etc... also on me.

INSTRUCTIONS FOR ENTRY:
- *When you arrive, take the Hotel entry on the opposite side of the Green Park tube station [Please refer to your arrival time at the end of this email]*
- *When asked 'how can I help you Sir/Madame?', you reply 'I am here for Lucy's Birthday Party at the Rivoli Bar'*

- *You will be escorted to the lounge area next to the Rivoli Bar, where you will hopefully see a gorgeous group of ladies.*
- *If you experience any issues getting in or getting to the Ritz, please call my mobile... and my PA Ms Gill will kindly deal with your queries between 8:30pm to 10pm.*

STRICT DRESS CODE:
- *Gentlemen: Jacket, shirt, and please also bring a tie (no jeans, trainers, flip-flops, polo-shirts) Ladies: skirt/top, cocktail dress (no denim, mini-skirts, flip-flops, bad tastes)*
- *Advice 1: It goes without saying that the more upper-class you dress, the less likely you shall be denied entry.*
- *Advice 2: Photos will be taken between 10pm to 10:30pm, and these will be distributed once processed, therefore you may want to be well-groomed! ;)*
- *Finally... I will be accepting cards and small gifts between 9pm to 11pm... hehehe*

- *I very much look forward to seeing you all at the Ritz this Friday.*

Lucy

ARRIVAL TIMES:
[Please stick to these as best as you can, thank you]

- *9:00pm: Lucy, Sophie Sandner, Kajai, Mandeep, Preet, Sanami, Su, Lisa, Kate.*
- *9:15pm: Phoebe, Sophie Seugnet, Theo, Dmitry, Ed, Nikolay, Paul, Nick, Harry.*
- *9:30pm: Marco, Andrea, Jess, Ovi, Yuki, Olga, Kim, Marcelo, Ulyana, Krystal, Dan.*
- *9:45pm: Sunita, Alan, JingJing, Emma.*
- *10:00pm: Anthony, Rachel, Roger, Uli, Yogi, Gharzi.*

Within hours this email had circulated around Citigroup and within days it had found its way around the globe, collecting further amused commentary on its way.

'How are your interns doing this summer?' wondered a director at UBS. 'Looks like Citi real estate research rocks!'

Another wrote, 'And I thought I was a control freak.'

This one really ran and ran, with newspapers quick to poke fun. WHAT A SILLY GAO, tittered *The Times*; SHE'S TAKING THE RITZ, enthused the *Evening Standard*; while the *Express* described her message as AN INVITATION TO BECOME A LAUGHING STOCK.

A spokeswoman for Citigroup managed to be less than fierce in her support when she told reporters that Lucy 'hasn't done anything wrong. It's just... she has everyone's sympathy.'

Gao's direct line at the Citigroup offices was quickly disconnected. Sadly for her, she had included her mobile phone number in the original email. She wisely switched it off when she realised that her message had a global audience and her voicemail box reached capacity almost immediately as people rang up to mock her.

As the world laughed its arse off at her message, Gao went into hiding. However, she appeared to be attempting to make amends via email:

Hi, fellow Citigroup interns. Just to clear a few things up, now that it is seriously getting out of control, it was suppose[d] to be an internal joke between me and a couple of my guests to my 21st Party.

I should not have used my Citigroup email account in the first place so I apologise for that. I am sorry if you found the content of the invitation details offensive and I am glad to entertain.

But please stop now because it is getting really unprofessional and unnecessary.

But Gao was soon the recipient of further honours. First was a spoof of her email, which was published in a newspaper diary column.

'You are cordially invited to my birthday party in McDonald's Brixton,' it began. 'Please get there early to avoid missing out on the buy-one-get-one-free cheeseburger offer. I will pay for your ketchup, you will only get one tub between two.

'Dress code: The more upper class you dress, the more likely you are to get mugged. You will be welcomed outside McDonald's by a tramp sitting by the entrance, pretending to play the harmonica.

'Entertainment will be provided courtesy of the Metropolitan Police, who will be escorting a group of Asbo Kids out on a day trip. McDonald's have arranged for a lovely angel cake for us to look at. PLEASE DO NOT TOUCH THE CAKE... You touch, you buy!'

The second honour came in the form of a T-shirt. The website cafepress.com produced two T-shirts in honour of Gao's email. One read: 'Lucy Gao kicked me out of the Ritz (I arrived at 9.01pm)' and another read: 'I survived Lucy Gao's 21st birthday party'. The T-shirts cost £9 each.

Thirdly, Gao's email was linked to a drop in trading. *The Financial Times* reported, in the wake of her message, 'In the wider market, it was an extremely quiet session ahead of the long holiday weekend. A trifling 1.8bn shares changed hands, with City dealers seemingly more interested in the latest e-mail from Lucy Gao, a Citigroup intern, than share price or index movements.'

As she became a short-term celebrity thanks

to her email, Gao cropped up on the website YouTube, where an Oxford University video was posted. It featured Gao and her friends discussing the delights of studying engineering at Oxford University. This video was evidently filmed before Gao's email disaster and it is interesting to see her happy and carefree, blissfully unaware of the humiliation that fate has in store for her. At the end of the video, the song 'Walking On Sunshine' by Katrina and The Waves is played and Gao treats viewers to a little dance. The song asks if it feels good, as she jives away happily.

Man with enormous cock

Charlie Phillips worked for Enron as an IT consultant and it was technology that brought about his downfall. The 34-year-old Devon man sent an email to his workmates with the subject line 'Man with an enormous cock'. The email contained a photo of a man with a very large chicken.

Although he only received a slap on the wrist from his bosses, Phillips says that, when his contract expired two months later, it was not renewed. He insists that most of his colleagues found the email amusing.

It was just a coincidence!

When journalist and former *Mirror* editor Piers Morgan was investigated by both the Department of Trade and Industry and the Press Complaints Commission, he found that his emails were produced as evidence against him.

Morgan insisted that it was a coincidence that the *Mirror* had tipped shares in technology company Viglen on the day after he had bought thousands of pounds' worth of shares in the company. However, the DTI was shown an email that Morgan sent to Anil Bhoyrul, editor of the *Mirror*'s City Slickers page. The message was sent on 17 January and showed that Morgan had told Bhoyrul of his Viglen purchase. No charges were brought against Morgan by the DTI.

After his jump, the dreadlocked man is seen being decapitated on some railings

Don't you just love it when people put an overly positive spin on something? Such as: 'Through this investigation we have been able to clearly restate the high standards of conduct required from everyone who works for us – this is no less than our public should expect and demand from us.'

Given what Deputy Chief Constable Simon Ash was discussing when he made the above statement, it is surprising that he was able to put such a happy face on it. He was referring to the investigation that led to no fewer than 140 Hertfordshire police officers and civilian staff being disciplined after a controversial email episode.

The email had originated in America and consisted of a video featuring a series of images showing a black man being chased by police and then jumping off a flyover. After his jump, the dreadlocked man is seen being decapitated on some railings. The email was distributed by officers in the force and, when bosses discovered this, they mounted what they described as a 'robust' five-month investigation.

They found that 400 Hertfordshire police officers and staff had received the email. Three hundred of these wisely deleted it but the other 100 forwarded it on to other people. All of these

100 were disciplined – among them eight police officers who were given a formal reprimand and seven who were given written warnings.

Two years previously, a similar scandal had rocked the Merseyside police force. A random inspection of computers at the force's headquarters found a host of racist, sexist, homophobic and pornographic messages.

Please be really really really really careful

I am told the following email is genuine and was sent out to staff at a real company. I haven't been able to come up with solid evidence of its veracity, but frankly it deserves inclusion anyway.

To: All Staff
Subject: Copier
Please, please please please please – I am begging – keep any and all paper clips away from the copier!

We have had two service calls in the last few days removing paper clips, staples and a binder clip from the innards of the copier.

PLEASE be really really really really careful around the copier. Especially the document handler, which seems to suck clits like a vacuum cleaner.

Thanks for your help.

There's not a lot I can add to that.

It was never intended to get this big

Anyone who was planning a party in December 2006 would have been delighted to receive a voucher that offered a whopping great 40 per cent discount on wine and champagne. The off-licence chain Thresher was offering this generous discount but had not intended it to be taken up quite as widely as it was.

The voucher was originally emailed by Thresher to a small South African winery. It was meant as a thank-you gesture to their suppliers, and included a line saying, 'Feel free to send it to your friends and family.' However, once the voucher entered cyberspace, it snowballed out of all control and was quickly downloaded by over half a million people. 'It was never intended to get this big,' said a spokesperson.

He added, 'We are scratching our heads vigorously, wondering how we can meet this level of demand and we are waiting with bated breath to see just how many customers take advantage of the discount and what it will mean for us financially.'

Fortunately, there was a £500 limit in the small print of the voucher.

The Thresher group – which includes Victoria Wine, Bottoms Up, Haddows, The Local and Wine Rack – promised to honour all vouchers at its 2,000 stores until the expiry date. As the email did the rounds and people realised that here was a chance to get drunk very cheaply, so many people used the Thresher website store locator facility that the website kept crashing.

The company admitted it was worried but also predicted that it could still make a profit on the offer. Through its 'buy two, get one free' offer, Thresher was already effectively offering a 33 per cent discount on wine and champagne, so the voucher only amounted to an extra 7 per cent off. Combine that with the fact that the chain got huge free publicity from the story and would claim the email address of any customer taking advantage of it and you wonder whether this was a great email disaster or a great email marketing coup.

Other stores including Selfridges, Gap, Borders, Urban Outfitters, Ted Baker, Coast and Kurt Geiger were soon getting in on the act. As Thresher's shelves were being emptied, so a nation's inboxes were getting jammed full of offers from other shops. Disaster or master-stroke, the Thresher episode is likely to change the way stores market themselves to us at Christmas forever.

CHAPTER SEVEN

AMERICAN NIGHTMARES

Anyone with a young daughter who uses the internet would be justifiably concerned about what sort of chats she might be having online. However, few mothers could imagine that their daughter would receive what 15-year-old Claire McDonald from Exmouth in Devon was sent – up to 11 times a week – by a man in America.

Please stop sending me these emails!

Royal Navy commander Jim Dale worked at the Pentagon in Washington and regularly emailed another Royal Navy commander in London. The contents of these emails included discussion of communications problems on the British warships the *Invincible* and *Illustrious*. They also chewed over software programs being tested by the British and American navies. Another topic of discussion was how the UK could keep sensitive military details secret.

These emails were also sent to schoolgirl Claire McDonald. She quickly told her mum and the pair alerted the Navy of the breach in security. However, Jim Dale replied saying that there must be a problem with her internet service provider. McDonald estimates that she must have received 250 different naval secrets before the problem was rectified. Her computer got so full of files as a result that it crashed.

Cute butt bouncing up and down

Republican congressman Mark Foley was once the chairman of the House Caucus on Missing and Exploited Children. He oversaw the introduction of legislation which targeted sexual predators. So it is with mammoth irony that we discover that Foley himself has been accused of behaving inappropriately with teenage boys.

The 2006 mid-term elections saw George W Bush's Republican Party absolutely walloped at the polls. The war in Iraq was correctly identified as the main cause of the Republicans' poor showing but the scandal that engulfed Foley just weeks before the polling was also a contributory factor.

Five weeks before the election, Mark Foley resigned from his safe seat in Florida's West Palm Beach, after it emerged he had sent inappropriate emails and instant messages to boys working as pages on Capitol Hill.

In these messages, Foley allegedly asked one young man to email him a photograph of himself and then asked him what he wanted for his birthday. More damaging were reports that Foley had offered one page the chance to stay at his house in return for oral sex and that he had emailed another requesting a photograph of his erect penis.

Before long, former pages were coming forward with allegations that Foley took part in inappropriate conversations with them over instant messaging. In one exchange, in which Foley used the username 'Maf54', the following exchange about masturbation took place:

> Maf54: *do you really do it face down*
> Teen: *ya*
> Maf54: *kneeling*
> Teen: *well i dont use my hand... i use the bed itself*
> Maf54: *where do you unload it*
> Teen: *towel*
> Maf54: *really*
> Maf54: *completely naked?*
> Teen: *well ya*
> Maf54: *very nice*
> Teen: *lol*
> Maf54: *cute butt bouncing in the air*

When these stories became public, Foley resigned and said, 'I am deeply sorry and I apologise for letting down my family and the people of Florida I have had the privilege to represent.' He then checked into a rehabilitation clinic for alcoholism.

I hope you'll indulge my wifely pride

There are many traditions in US politics and one of them is that speechwriters who work with the President remain anonymous and never claim credit for the words they put in the leader's smouth. Canadian David Frum was a hugely successful and popular figure in the White House, but lost his job thanks to an email slip by his wife.

When George W Bush coined the term 'axis of evil' in his state of the union address, it grabbed the attention of the media around the world. The phrase was dreamed up by speechwriter Frum, and his wife Danielle was rightly proud of her husband's success.

However, it was deeply unfortunate that she breached the speechwriters' code by sending this email to 15 of her friends: 'I realise this is very "Washington" of me to mention but my husband is responsible for the axis of evil segment in Tuesday's state of the union address. It's not often a phrase one writes gains national notice... so I hope you'll indulge my wifely pride in seeing this one repeated in headlines everywhere!'

It was even less fortunate that this email then came to the notice of the media. It was claimed on CNN that when Bush learned of this he fired Frum. Others claimed that, when he discovered what his wife had done, Frum jumped before he was pushed. As for Frum, he insists that he gave a month's notice while the speech was still being written and before any of the controversy kicked off.

Three days before he was inaugurated as President of the United States of America, George W Bush sent a final email to his friends. It read: 'Since I do not want my private conversations looked at by those out to embarrass, the only course of action is not to correspond in cyberspace.'

Smart words and ones that should have been heeded by more of his staff. When it came to Bush's re-election, two leaked emails raised questions over the legitimacy of his victory. BBC's *Newsnight* produced two messages which had been sent to the executive director of the Bush campaign in Florida and the national research director in Washington. The messages included a 15-page list of 1,886 names and addresses of voters in Jacksonville, Florida. The majority of these voters were black, Democratic supporters and it was suggested that the list had been drawn up so Bush's people could challenge their right to vote.

Bush has since reaffirmed his distrust of email as a communication tool. In a speech to the American Society of Newspaper Editors, he said he had given up using email to prevent 'personal stuff' being leaked. 'I've made an easy decision there,' he said. 'I just don't do it. Which is sad, really, when you think about it.'

Soon after this, US Attorney General Alberto Gonzales announced that he has given up cyberspace communication for the same reason: 'I don't get email and I don't send email.'

A *neat idea*

If you are going to get involved in political issues where you really should remain neutral, then discretion is definitely advisable every time you switch your computer on. But if you are going to get involved with the clandestine sale of weapons to Iran to support Contras in Nicaragua, or you are a White House intern having an affair with the married President of the United States of America, then discretion is mandatory at all times.

Everything is bigger in America: the skyscrapers, the cities and the food helpings. The cyber slip-ups made in the world of American politics are also that much bigger. Oliver North found himself in the middle of a huge political scandal when he was a member of Ronald Reagan's administration and was accused of clandestinely selling weapons to Iraq to raise funds to support the Contra rebel group in Nicaragua.

It was a serious accusation and one he'd have found far easier to counter had he not, on 23 August 1986, sent an email in which he outlined his illegal plan. He had struck a deal with Panama President Manuel Noriega that if the US lifted the ban on arms sales to the Panama Defence Force then Noriega would 'take care' of Nicaragua's left-wing Sandinista leadership in return. However, Noriega would also require funds for this venture and, North suggested, these could be raised by selling US arms to Iran.

North described his plan as a 'neat idea'. Not

that neat, Oliver. He was fired by Reagan and summoned to testify in front of a joint Congressional committee. He was indicted on 16 felony counts and convicted of three. He was then sentenced to a three-year suspended prison sentence, $150,000 in fines and 1,200 hours' community service.

After a series of appeals, his convictions were eventually overturned but his career was in ruins as a result of his email indiscretion. Before leaving North's case, let's reflect that the man who thought his Iran-Contra plan was a 'neat idea' clearly had a slightly leftfield idea of what constituted a neat idea. This is the man who, when he visited Iranian leader Ayatollah Khomeini, took as gifts to the hardline Islamic leader a chocolate cake and a Bible.

More recently, a person – identity unknown – accidentally sent a text message to Mahmoud Ahmadinejad, the current Iranian President, poking fun at his alleged lack of personal hygiene. You can only imagine the fear deep in the bowels of the texter when he or she realised their mistake. This is the man, after all, who has threatened to wipe Israel off the map. Of all the communication cock-ups to make, sending a joke mocking one of the world's leading big boys was surely an extremely unwise one.

I want to hug him so bad right now I could cry

Bill Clinton describes his affair with former White House intern Monica Lewinsky as 'a terrible mistake'. Certainly, as the pair's dirty washing really was hung out for all to see, Clinton must have had cause for regret. However, along with Lewinsky's semen-stained dress, a series of emails were also made public during the investigation into the affair.

During her subsequent time in the Pentagon's public affairs office, Lewinsky – who was continuing to visit Clinton – became close to another employee there, Linda Tripp. As well as secretly recording telephone conversations between them, Tripp also saved some emails that Lewinsky had sent her, in which Lewinsky described Clinton as 'the creep'.

In one such email, Lewinsky complains, 'The big creep didn't even try to call me on V-Day [Valentine's Day].'

Another email read: 'I will be checking my messages in the hopes that the creep will call and say "Thank you for my love note. I love you. Will you run away with me?" What do ya think the likelihood of that happening is?'

Another read: 'I want to hug him so bad right now I could cry.'

Clinton was – for obvious reasons – trying to find Lewinsky a job away from Washington where the glare of the media was homing in on the pair. In one email during this period, Lewinsky described a meeting with 'the big creep's best friend' which was a reference to one of Clinton's aides.

The email read: 'He said, with regard to my job search, 'You're in business.' He also said the creep had talked to him, and as I was leaving he said, "You come highly recommended." Tee hee hee.'

Tripp handed the emails over to Kenneth Starr who was heading the investigation. This did nothing for her popularity and many Americans decided that she was as much of a creep as Clinton.

'They were things that I thought I had deleted,' Lewinsky said of the emails. 'I certainly came to see that obviously I was wrong. While you may think it's deleted, it isn't. I mean it's there permanently.

'That's also the same with some of the internet providers – they keep a copy of everything you send. You may think something is not trackable and it is.'

The experience, Lewinsky says, cost her dearly: 'I think privacy is sort of one of those things that you don't think about until it's been violated, a bit like anonymity.'

She adds, 'I think there isn't enough information out there for people who are on the internet to be fully aware of exactly what they can be getting themselves into.'

Lewinsky says she rarely uses email for anything other than work now. 'I think maybe in a few years, when I feel that my life is sort of all my own, I might feel more comfortable.'

There were some issues of poor judgement that impaired his ability to lead going forward

Harry Stonecipher was once Boeing's president and chief executive but he resigned in March

2005 after reports that he had cheated on his wife with a female Boeing executive. Boeing had ruled that his behaviour was 'inconsistent with Boeing's Code of Conduct' and 'would impair his ability to lead the company'. His wife filed for divorce just days later.

Stonecipher's downfall came about in part because of a series of steamy emails between him and his mistress. The Boeing investigation found that the affair had only lasted a few weeks, but that was not enough to save Stonecipher's job or his marriage. 'It's not the fact that he was having an affair' that caused him to be fired, a spokesman told reporters. 'But as we explored the circumstances surrounding the affair, we just thought there were some issues of poor judgement that ... impaired his ability to lead going forward.'

Ironically, Stonecipher had only returned to Boeing as the result of their former chief financial officer losing his job due to email indiscretion. Michael Sears was found to have offered a job to Darleen Druyun who, as someone with influence in US Air Force acquisition, would still have had sway over contracts involving Boeing.

Sears was busted partly as the result of an email he wrote about his meeting with Druyun. He was fired in 2003 and later sentenced to four months' imprisonment and fined $250,000 after admitting breaking conflict of interest laws. Druyun had earlier received a nine-month sentence for favouring Boeing when awarding lucrative contracts.

Oops, I haven't beaten anyone that bad in a long time

If you are a policeman and you are battering a suspect with batons until his skull is fractured and he suffers other internal injuries, it is best to check that a bystander is not videoing the entire incident. However, in 1991, officers of the Los Angeles Police Department were caught on camera beating Rodney King and within 24 hours the video was being broadcast around the world. Just as the footage helped bring the policemen down, so did a computer message.

King was pulled over by LAPD officers after a high-speed chase. He had been drinking and his driving was erratic. Four officers ordered King out of his car and beat him repeatedly with their batons. They claimed they had acted in self-defence. However, others claimed that their assault on King was racially motivated and the case was used to highlight the racism and poverty suffered by the black community in South Central Los Angeles.

When the officers were brought to trial on charges of assault, the court heard that one of them, Laurence Powell, had sent out computer messages prior to and following the incident. The message he had sent out prior to the arrest referred to a domestic incident involving a black family. He compared the scene to 'Gorillas in the Mist'. One of his post-beating messages read: 'Oops, I haven't beaten anyone that bad in a long time.'

Although the four were initially found not guilty – sparking riots across the neighbour-hood that claimed the lives of 55 people and caused more than $1 billion of damage – a year later, they faced a second trial and two of them, including Powell, were sent to prison. Oops indeed.

SEX AND ROMANCE

(PART TWO)

There are some things that couples want to boast about. When a couple get engaged and then married, they want everyone to know. When they buy a house, they want to shout it from the rooftops. When they have a child, everybody is told. However, when a couple has phone-sex, they generally want to keep that to themselves, even though the details would be far more interesting than yet another scan of a foetus.

Speaking of wanking, how was yours?

Thank the Lord for Sharon Dyson. No, let's be

precise – thank the Lord for the 'reply all' function on email. Dyson, who worked for Hobsons, a student careers advice firm, and the 'reply all' came together to hugely entertaining effect when she was on a work trip in Australia. Her boyfriend Alex Hewson sent a 'round-robin' email to her and 30 other people. Dyson wrote a reply intended to go just to her boyfriend, but accidentally hit the 'reply all' button and sent the message to all 30 people on the list.

The email began harmlessly enough, with Dyson recounting how she had been shopping for some new clothes. However, she then took a bizarre turn and in just two paragraphs managed to insult her work clients, confess to dancing like a dickhead and describe the phone-sex sessions she and her boyfriend had been enjoying.

'I have a big week this week, wish me luck Alex cause I'll need it,' she wrote. 'My sunburn on my back is sore and I need you to rub moisturiser in for me. We'll have to get some massage oil too. I have to write a sucky "thank you" email to clients now, wank wank. Speaking of wanking, how was yours? Wish I could have been there to watch. You have made me cum a few times, not as good as the real thing but I guess we have to make do the best we can with what we've got.

'The band I saw last night were SO good. I danced like a dickhead and a 17-year-old tried to pick me up (well he must have been 19 to get in but looked about 15). Oh Alex, I so wanted you to be there to hold my hand, I love music. Smile beautiful, Sharon xoxo.'

The 30 accidental recipients must have been delighted with all this detail. Very soon, some of them had forwarded the message to their friends and, before long, people across the globe were reading all about the couple's phone sex and Dyson the dancing dickhead.

One recipient hit 'reply all' himself and wrote, 'Just a little note to say a very big thank you for livening up what was proving to be a very dull afternoon. People are talking about this being the best example of how to accidentally "reply to all". I mean, come on, I quote "Oh Alex, I so wanted you to be there to hold my hand, I love music." Who talks like that? What are you, like 16 or something?

'Alex you need to sort this out. If she is 16, you're in trouble. If she's not then you need to get rid of her asap before she takes over your life.'

For at least a while, the whole affair did indeed take over both partners' lives. As the message pinged around the world, it was inevitable that it would quickly come to the attention of Dyson's bosses as Hobsons. When it did, they were less than impressed by her disparaging remarks about the company's clients.

A spokeswoman for Hobsons told reporters, 'Ms Dyson is still employed. We will be dealing with it as a private staff matter. All emails sent are the view of individual members of staff and not representative of Hobsons. We have staff procedures in place to deal with any incidents of this nature.'

Whether 'incidents of this nature' meant general emails that go astray or specifically emails about phone-sex is not known. Meanwhile, Hewson admitted that he was embarrassed by the affair and that his employers were also less than pleased by it. He refused to go into it any further, saying, 'I can't make any comment at all about it. She's still out of the country.'

By the time that Dyson's business trip was over, she was something of a celebrity. When she flew back to the UK, journalists and photographers from the press were waiting to greet her at the airport. They knew that Hewson was due to meet her off the plane because in the email Dyson had written, 'Do you remember you said you'd pick me up from the airport???? ah ha now you've said it you'll have to go through with it.'

Reporters fired questions at the couple, including asking Hewson whether he had indeed bought the massage oil. They refused to answer any questions. The next day, newspapers excitedly boasted about having 'the first pictures of the saucy email lovers'. One journalist suggested that Dyson could have a great future in writing soft-porn stories.

Yours was yum

What was going through the mind of Bradley Chait when he decided to forward an email from his girlfriend, Claire Swire? Chait was a laddish,

27-year-old solicitor who charged £100 per hour for his time, but that didn't stop him having a moment of email madness.

He had received an email from his 26-year-old girlfriend which contained a few naughty jokes, including some references to what the popular press would term 'a sex act'. She complimented Chait on this aspect of their relationship and told him, 'Yours was yum.'

Unable to resist the temptation to boast about this, Chait forwarded the email to six of his friends, adding his own comment at the top, 'Now that's a nice compliment from a lass, isn't it?'

Indeed it is, but you can't help thinking that the lass would much rather he didn't share it with his closest friends.

She would have been even less keen on one of those friends, Edward Drummond, immediately forwarding the mail to 12 of his friends, with his own added line reading: 'Beggars belief. I feel honour-bound to circulate this.'

However, Swire's feelings were not going to stop this email now. It whizzed around computers across the globe, with new comments being attached along the way: 'What a top lass – let's start a campaign to find her!'; 'I know it's mean but v funny'; 'Chain of bastards to make this one public but funny anyway.'

The consequences for both Chait and Swire were immense. Newspaper journalists started to hunt them down and they were forced into hiding. Former work colleagues of Swire were quizzed. To 'do a Swire' was added to the list of synonyms for oral sex. A website dedicated to mocking the pair was set up. A soldier in Kosovo called in all his specialist contacts to try to hunt Swire down. The letterbox of her home in Fulham was bombarded with saucy Christmas cards.

Swire's parents – you have to feel for them – were tracked down and questioned by reporters. Her mother said, 'Claire is horrified by this. She has gone into hiding. Would you stick around after something like that? We're OK, we're dealing with it. We have things under control and we're sorting it all out.' Her father added, 'We can't believe how much interest this thing has caused.'

However, saying you have something under

control and actually keeping it under control are two very different things, particularly when it comes to the internet. The intrigue about the pair continued, with newspapers and website polls calling for Chait to be dismissed. The Law Society came to his aid, saying, 'From what we've heard, it doesn't sound like a breach of contract. We've never heard of lawyers being sacked for email abuse.'

However, nine City workers were suspended for forwarding the email and a spokesman for Chait's law firm, Norton Rose, said, 'Norton Rose takes a robust approach to email abuse. The firm has clear rules that specifically prohibit the sending and accepting of non-work-related material, in particular obscene, discriminatory or defamatory material and junk mail.'

A close friend of Swire – who worked for internet company magicbutton.net – said Swire felt 'humiliated' by the fiasco which she was finding 'dark'. Other friends painted a less depressing picture of Swire, describing her as a 'party-going Sloane'.

Meanwhile, the boss of *Playboy TV*

Jeremy Yates called for her to get in touch with him. 'We want to find her,' he dribbled. 'She would be the perfect person to host a show on sex topics for us.'

Mirror columnist Sue Carroll added to the fun: 'Claire's indiscretion could make her very rich. One can only hope she doesn't, er, blow it.' The same newspaper dubbed Chait a 'Brad boy', while the *Sun* called his girlfriend 'Yummy Claire'. Meanwhile, the *Evening Standard* said, 'It's time we all grew up'. No chance.

PR guru Max Clifford also stuck his oar in. 'From her email she sounds fun and lively,' he said. 'She clearly knows her own mind. It depends on her attitude, but if she comes across as an independent person with some interesting and original views on sex and relationships in the office, which she seems to have, you are talking about tens of thousands of pounds.

'Her misfortune really could be the launching pad to all kinds of things, especially because she sounds like she has a sense of humour as well. If she is capable of being that frank in public, then she would be perfect. If she wants to do a photo shoot, there might well be a chance of that.'

Any hopes of the story quietly fading away were dashed when the press discovered Claire was the second cousin of Hugo Swire, a director of Sotheby's who was hoping to become a Conservative candidate in a Devon constituency. It also transpired that she was related to Sir Adrian Swire, a super-rich shipping and trading magnate. Both men remained tight-lipped but a friend of the family told the press, 'They thought they'd got away with it. Of course, she is only a distant cousin, but it's still pretty mortifying.'

By this stage, over 10 million people were estimated to have read Swire's 'Yours was yum' email. Among them was Henry Liu, who lives in central China. 'Happy your Christmas,' he wrote to a friend in London. 'First, thank you so mush. Well, I found a new in internet about UK. A girl love with she's boyfriend (I can't spell them name) they are famous at the moment. The girl write done her best felt with her boyfriend love and send mail to she's boyfriend who got a mail was exciting it after that he send the mail to his six friends whom send the mail over the world.' His English may not be perfect but he sums the story up well, doesn't he?

Come dressed as porn stars, flashers and anything sleazy and cheesy

Rachael Fountain was very proud when she and her boyfriend Pascal Sharples were about to appear on television. So she emailed all her friends, inviting them to a party on the night of the show's transmission. So far, so good. However, the show in question was Channel 4's *Sex Tips For Girls* and the invitation featured a picture of a bunny girl and naked men. It invited guests to come dressed as 'porn stars, prossies, pimps, gimps, flashers, slutty schoolgirls and anything sleazy and cheesy'.

So, when she accidentally emailed the invitation to her boss, she was in real trouble. Fountain worked at American Express, where the finance director shared the same name as one of Fountain's friends.

'So when I typed in her name it must have taken the email address from the company address book and not my personal one,' explained Fountain. 'Apparently I'd sent the other woman things before, asking her for dinner and general chit-chat. You'd think she would have emailed me back to say I'd got the wrong person. She must have thought it was a bit odd.'

Fountain did not know of her mistake until the week after the party when she returned to work and was told she was suspended. While she was suspended, her email account was examined with a fine-tooth comb by her employers. She was particularly upset by this and compared it to them reading her diary. 'There were arguments with my boyfriend in there,' she sniffed.

She then received written confirmation that she had infringed the company's electronic communications policy 'by using Amex systems to send an inappropriate personal email'. She was sacked for gross misconduct.

'It was supposed to be a bit of fun,' said Fountain. 'Other managers at work knew about it and thought it was hilarious. It wasn't an orgy or anything, just a fancy-dress party. The invitation was tongue-in-cheek. Around 100 people turned up dressed as YMCA workmen, bunny girls, wearing flasher macs, that sort of thing. It was all a giggle.

'We had decorated the loft to look like a harem. The most saucy it got was when one friend brought along a bullwhip, and later we got the game Twister out. Not particularly dirty. But it wasn't a dirty evening.

'I was shocked when they told me what I'd done,' she said. 'The name of the finance director isn't particularly unusual but I still couldn't believe what happened. The woman obviously didn't see the funny side.'

However, since being sacked from her £12,000-a-year job at American Express, Fountain has had the last laugh. She became a professional model and earned far more than she ever did working in administration for American Express.

West Ham are on the box and Laura's on her knees sucking my piece

On 1 October 2002, West Ham United travelled to the Recreation Ground to play Chesterfield in the League Cup. Despite having the likes of Joe Cole, Paolo Di Canio, David James and Trevor Sinclair in their side, West Ham struggled to beat their less illustrious opponents. The match ended 1–1 after extra time and the match went to penalties. A tense penalty shoot-out ended with West Ham winning 5–4.

A reasonably eventful and memorable evening for West Ham fans, then. However, for one Hammer, it was to prove extremely memorable. Trevor Luxton, then 22, was a clerk for the bank Credit Lyonnais. His fiancée Jo was away for a few days and he had decided to spend the evening in front of the telly.

His account of how he did so proves that the young man who calls himself Luxyboy is 'a bit of a lad', at least in his own imagination. As well as the actual detail of his account, note how he drops in cockney rhyming slang, too: 'ruby' for curry (Ruby Murray) and 'dog' for phone (dog and bone). What a boy!

Luxyboy's message read: 'Last night I was all geared up for a night in front of the telly watching football, having a ruby and a couple of beers while Jo's still away.

'Suddenly, I get a text from Laura, my mate's ex, which says "I'm coming round because I need to see you". So she comes round and we get chatting about all sorts of stuff and then we start kissing and fondling (as you do).

'Then I find myself sitting in the armchair with a beer in one hand, remote in the other,

West Ham on the box and Laura on her knees sucking my piece. Then the phone rings and it's Jo who was bored at the airport.

'So now I've got my beer, Laura sucking and Jo chatting to me on the dog when Laura stops sucking, looks up at me, winks and whispers "Say hello to Jo for me" and then gets back to the job in hand. Am I the worst boyfriend in the world or what??????'

Beer, curry, football, cockney rhyming slang, extra-curricular sex – no wonder he wanted to boast to his mates! So he sent the message to five equally laddish-sounding friends called Chris, Kev, Rog, Sarts and Tony at 9.20am the following day. Within four minutes, Tony had forwarded the message to a friend of his in the City. From there it spread like wildfire reaching computer terminals at the Bank of England, Bloomberg, HSBC, Logica, the Football Association, Emap, Parthenon Entertainment, KPMG Durlacher, Barclays and Capital Management Group.

The commentary on the forwarded message revealed the motivations of many of the forwarders. 'Let's nail the dirty love rat,' said one.

'Let's get his two-timing arsehole in trouble – send this to everyone you know who works in the City and hopefully it will get back to his bird,' roared another.

As the email whizzed around the world, Luxyboy realised he was in serious trouble. As one newspaper columnist wrote, it is tempting to think that his first words on realising his mistake were 'Blow me!' Dubbed THE SEX EMAIL TWIT by the *Sun*, he was suspended on full pay as his employers investigated him. He was quizzed by a director and by human resources bosses.

Meanwhile, his fiancée Jo Kivlehan was naturally devastated, though the pair met up to try and salvage their relationship.

As her father told reporters, 'She is naturally very upset but they are very much still together. They are trying to sort something out amicably.'

Her mother added, 'Our lives have been ruined by this.'

Luxton's dad, meanwhile, said, 'A mate let him down,' and his mother admitted, 'He is worried that he will lose his job. He is very worried about the mortgage.'

The two sets of parents met up to discuss

the matter. One can only imagine how the conversation went!

Thomas, however, was shouting and screaming her innocence, claiming that Luxton invented the whole episode. 'I did not do it. I wasn't even round there,' she insisted. Eventually, Luxton also denied the incident took place and claimed he'd made it up after reading a similar story in a lads' magazine. (A lads' mag! What a geezer!)

Not that these denials were enough to stop the world from reading and laughing at his fate. T-shirts went on sale on the internet for £12 with 'Clever Trevor' emblazoned across the front together with the text of his email. Even worse news for Luxyboy was that his premonition that he'd lose his job proved correct. Following their investigation, Credit Lyonnais confirmed that it had 'accepted his resignation'.

It was rumoured that he would receive a full year's pay in return but any consolation he might have found in this was probably wiped out by Laura's subsequent quotes in the press. 'Trevor is a pathetic prat,' she stormed. 'He couldn't accept I didn't want to have sex with him.'

Not silly boy anymore!

One man who might rival Luxyboy in the laddish stakes is investment banker Robert Imlah. The corporate finance analyst sent a string of emails boasting about sexual conquests he had been enjoying.

In one email he boasted about a new lover of his, and one of his friends asked if he had gone 'bare back' when he had slept with her. Imlah replied, 'No mate, bagged up! Not silly boy anymore! Banging Lauren tonight as well, prob won't bag up there!! ... It's all about the numbers not the figures! Ha ha ha!'

These emails were sent between Imlah and his friends, who were mostly former football team-mates from his home town of Peterborough enjoying the kind of conversations that lads typically have. However, Imlah was feeling less than laddish when the emails – which were sent from his work account at investment bank JP Morgan – were somehow forwarded around the world. As they circulated across computer screens, they built up their own commentary from everyone

who read them. One said they proved that 'men
are vile'.

Imlah was suspended from JP Morgan, whose
spokesman said, 'We take a very dim view of this
kind of thing and we are investigating.'

Mr Football? Do you mean the coach? He is on my case BIG time!

Another scandal involving football, sex and email
almost brought down the Football Association, the
game's governing body. Faria Alam was working
as a secretary at the FA when a woman from her
past began emailing her. The woman knew Alam
from her modelling days 10 years previously. She
had long suspected that Alam had slept with her
partner and so – posing as an old school friend –
decided to start emailing Alam and ask questions
of her love life.

Using the name Laila Khan, the woman
pretended she had been at the same school as
Alam and introduced herself via the Friends
Reunited website. Alam apologised for not
remembering 'Khan' but soon the pair were
swapping saucy emails about their sex lives.
At one point, Alam even made an unflattering

reference to her real-life rival turned cyber correspondent. She wrote, 'Darling, trust me – she is not at all beautiful. Shall I tell you why he fell for her... because she had green eyes... nothing more... she was also quite a bitch to him.'

Ouch! However, the correspondence continued and, before long, Alam was emailing tips for oral sex and details of a lesbian encounter. 'I don't regret it – I loved it, enjoyed it thoroughly – this girl was brilliant and I had a blast doing it – I DON'T CARE! – BUT – I will say this much... I MUCH PREFER MEN! ANY DAY!'

Indeed she does, as more than one of the staff at the FA was discovering. Within two and a half weeks of their correspondence beginning, Alam was spilling the beans about the saucy goings-on at the FA's Soho Square headquarters.

First, she admitted that she had slept with chief executive Mark Palios. 'The sex was fantastic... very passionate.' Her correspondent then asked about Sven-Göran Eriksson, to which Alam replied, 'Mr Football? Do you mean the coach? No... although he is on my case BIG time!'

She then wrote more about Palios. 'There is SOMETHING going on – we're not just termed as "a friend". I know he really likes me, he holds me as if he's held a woman for the first time – the thing with me is I need to feel needed... whatever it is, it's nothing as bad as I feel great.'

She nicknamed Palios Pretty Polly or PP and she outlined a dinner date the pair had been on. She said, 'It's not that I'm even in love with PP – I just like him a lot that's all.'

Turning back to Sven – who she nicknamed Sugar and described as a 'generous lover' – she wrote, 'Haven't been naughty, yet, but the guy I will see tomorrow night is the more famous one. Let's call him Sugar, he's very sweet and he's the coach.

'I'm 36, unmarried and loving it. My social life is amazing. I date famous people though I'm not at liberty to name them.

'Sugar is brilliant... I want to be very, very rich and successful and I will be. I'm not going to be going through life settling for second best in life, ever. If all goes well with Sugar we'll have to announce it to the papers.'

Earlier in the same week that these emails

were revealed, the FA had denied any such affairs had taken place. Faced with the evidence of the emails, it was forced to backtrack.

The FA statement said, 'Earlier in the week the Football Association made statements on behalf of Faria Alam, denying that she had a sexual relationship with the England coach Sven-Göran Eriksson.

'New evidence has been presented to us in the form of emails which Ms Alam has sent to friends about the relationship and, having made further enquiries, we can confirm that a relationship did take place.'

Alam resigned and then took the FA to an employment tribunal, claiming unfair dismissal, breach of contract and sexual discrimination. She claims that she only resigned because her position had been made untenable and that she had therefore effectively been dismissed. The emails were read out during the tribunal and further claims were made by Alam about another member of the FA.

The tribunal rejected her case but Alam was able to make hundreds of thousands of pounds by selling her story with the help of PR guru

Max Clifford. She later appeared on *Celebrity Big Brother*. While in the house, she claimed that she had once urinated in the tea of a lover. (How classy.) During her eviction interview, she was asked if that lover was Eriksson. She shook her head.

Oh, by the way ... someone's gotta start Fedexing me boxes of condoms

Life was good for New York trader Peter Chung in 2001. A graduate of top American university Princeton, he had moved from investment bank Merrill Lynch to join global investors Carlyle, who sent him to work in their branch in Seoul, South Korea. He enjoyed, so he says, a colourful social and private life in Seoul, and couldn't wait to boast to his pals back in New York.

His email was entitled 'Live like a king' and read:

So I've been in Korea for about a week and a half now and what can I say, life is good. The main bedroom is for my queen size bed where Chung is going to xxxx every hot chick in Korea over the next two years (5 down, 1,000,000,000 left to go), the second bedroom is for my harem of chickies, and the third bedroom is for all of you xxxxxx when you come out to visit my ass in Korea.

I go out to Korea's finest clubs, bars and lounges pretty much every other night on the weekdays and everyday on the weekends. I know I was a stud but I pretty much get about, on average, 5–8 phone numbers a night and at least 3 hot chicks that say that they want to go home with me every night I go out.

Oh, by the way ... someone's gotta start Fedexing me boxes of condoms ... I brought about 40 but I think I'll run out of them by Saturday. Laters, Chung

He sent this colourful email to 11 people but, sadly for Chung, one of the recipients was so annoyed by his immature boasting that he forwarded it on to many more people, including powerful figures at leading financial institutions Lehman Brothers, JP Morgan and Goldman, Sachs & Co.

The initial forwarder added his own note: 'Lock, stock and one blazing moron'.

As it was forwarded around the world, it collected new comments including: 'This guy ranks among the all-time classics' and 'He is the laughing stock of the world'. One of his former work colleagues then began to circulate a photograph of Chung.

The laughing stock of the world had also included his mobile-phone number at the bottom of the email, so he was quickly made aware of the scale of his error. Two days later, he chucked in his £100,000-a-year job. The *Daily Mail* dubbed him the TRADER WHO TRADED HIMSELF OUT OF A JOB.

'He felt he should resign after discovering the email had been so widely circulated,' said a Carlyle spokesman.

Life can be a bit boring here

They are a randy bunch over at the Driver and Vehicle Licensing Agency in Swansea. In 2006, 14 staff were sacked for distributing hardcore pornography via their office email accounts. 'It is everywhere, it is hardcore and very offensive,' said one disgruntled recipient.

The same agency had previously hit the headlines for firing Heather Muirhead who used her mobile phone to film herself having sex with her boyfriend Lee Jones at a Travelodge hotel in Swansea.

The romp took place after the pair had downed two bottles of wine and eight cans of lager and was recorded on Muirhead's mobile phone. She was accused of sending clips of the romp to friends at the DVLA office, but Muirhead claimed the clips must have been sent out after someone borrowed her phone from her desk.

What is certain, though, is that very quickly hundreds of staff at the DVLA had seen the clip. 'It soon snowballed, which is not that surprising. Life can be a bit boring here,' said one employee.

Another added, 'It started out as a bit of a joke but it got out of hand. It shows how careful you have to be with new technology.'

Indeed. At the last count, Jones reckons that at least 5,000 people have now seen footage of his hotel romp.

When the 14 staff were sacked for sending porn, one blogger came up with the heading 'Mirror, signal... er, masturbate.'

As a result of the agency's investigations

into the porn, 101 staff were disciplined by their managers. Given the goings-on at the DVLA, you can't help thinking they enjoyed the experience.

Some mistakes are bigger than others

It is easy to feel sorry for Heather and her boyfriend over the stick they received after filming their romp on a mobile phone. However, it is impossible to feel at all sorry for Gary Richards, who used his phone to take intimate photographs that came back to haunt him.

Richards, then 48, was a college welfare officer and also ran mini-football tournaments for children. After he sexually abused two 14-year-old girls, he was caught when his 15-year-old daughter found naked images of one of the girls on her father's mobile phone.

He was jailed for two years at Salisbury Crown Court after admitting to six counts of inciting children under 16 to engage in sexual activity and one of sexual activity with a child under 16. 'People make mistakes,' said his daughter after he was jailed. 'It's just some are bigger than others.'

CHAPTER NINE

BLOGS AND BUFFOONS

On 4 November 2002, a high-school pupil from Trois-Rivieres, Quebec, made a video of himself mucking around. Little did he know that, within months, the video would make him a reluctant internet celebrity and lead to him receiving psychiatric care.

Hey! It's the Star Wars Kid

The video featured Ghyslain Raza swinging a golf ball retriever around, pretending it was a weapon. He seemed to be trying to emulate the movement of Darth Maul from the *Star Wars* series. He filmed the video in the studio of his school but soon forgot about it, leaving the video tape in the basement of the school.

Some months later, a fellow pupil discovered the tape and, together with four friends, uploaded it on to the Kazaa online file-sharing system so he could show it to a few friends. However, the sharing quickly went beyond just the friends. The clip quickly became hugely popular and was downloaded by millions. As the cult of the '*Star Wars* kid' clip grew, so did more and more edited versions of the clip appear. *Star Wars* music was added, as was the sound of a light-sabre.

Raza quickly became a celebrity. The video clip was referenced in more than 10 television shows around the globe. An internet petition was opened to try and secure him a cameo role in the next instalment of the *Star Wars* series. When an online whip-round was organised to buy Raza an iPod, thousands of dollars were raised within a week.

However, Raza was not enjoying his newfound fame. His family filed a lawsuit against the families of the four classmates who posted the clip online. The lawsuit stated that, because of the video's distribution, Raza had endured harassment and derision from schoolmates and the general public. It also claimed that he had been teased so much that he had dropped out of school and needed psychological treatment.

'It was unbearable, totally. It was impossible to attend class,' he said. He also said that, wherever he went in public, strangers would mock him about the video. They would shout, 'Hey! It's Ghyslain Raza! *Star Wars* kid, hey!'

Proceedings against one of the families were dropped and then, in April 2006, it was revealed that his family had reached an out-of-court settlement with the families of his former classmates. At the last count, the video had been viewed over 900 million times, making it the most watched 'viral' email video of all time.

Impossible Is Nothing

One video that cannot be far behind the *Star Wars* kid in the most-viewed stakes is the one made by Aleksey Vayner. Born Aleksey Garber in Uzbekistan, Vayner was a Yale University student who emailed his CV to the UBS Bank in search of work. Alongside his 11-page CV was a short video entitled *Impossible Is Nothing*.

A triumph of pomposity and lack of self-awareness, the video would probably even make *The Office*'s David Brent blush. It includes footage of him lifting free weights which he claims weigh 140lbs each. He is then shown bench-pressing and serving a tennis ball: this time a caption claims that the speed of the serve is 140mph. He is also filmed karate-chopping a pile of bricks. What a man! However, to show that he has a gentle side too, Vayner also appears taking ballroom-dancing lessons.

But the video's crowning glory is Vayner's running commentary, in which he expands on his philosophies on life and success. It begins with an offscreen interviewer telling Vayner that he has become 'a model of personal development and an inspiration to many around you'.

Vayner manages a shy smile at this line and says, 'Well, thank you.'

He then embarks on a spectacularly pompous monologue including such nuggets of wisdom as the revelation that your physical fitness levels are reflected in your energy levels. He dismisses the idea that successful people are lucky. 'I completely disagree with that notion,' he sneers before brushing aside other notions held by 'the average observer'. He recounts how tennis coaches told him he would never be able to serve and laughs to himself, as footage of his 140mph serve is shown.

'Failure cannot be considered an option,' he says. 'To achieve success, you must first conceive it and believe in it.'

In the accompanying CV, Vayner told his prospective UBS employers that their 'reputation as one of the top investment management firms in the world motivates me to consider a career with your firm'. Lucky them!

Unfortunately for Vayner, someone at UBS was motivated to consider forwarding the video to friends. Very quickly, the video was posted on the internet and being watched by hundreds of thousands of people around the world. It was soon being discussed widely in the media, with everyone from *Fox News*, *The New York Times*, the *Sun* and the *Daily Mail* reporting on it.

Vayner made legal threats against YouTube and other websites hosting the video. He also confirmed that he was considering suing UBS, saying he had been extensively harassed as a result of the leaking of the video.

Better news came from Donny Deutsch, an advertising executive, who said he would happily hire Vayner having seen the video.

A viewer on YouTube went one further: 'I think the USA has found its new President.'

I felt like I disappointed God

Catherine Bosley was a newsreader at US news station WKBN in Youngstown, Ohio, for a decade. So she should have known better than to be making the news by taking part in a wet T-shirt competition. While taking a break in Key West in Florida in 2004, Bosley paraded around on a stage in a wet T-shirt. She then stripped down to her shorts, then just a thong and finally took that off so she was totally naked.

As the crowd cheered her every move, one audience member was filming her entire routine. The video was then posted online. Soon, thousands were enjoying the footage but Bosley's bosses were not among them. They accused her of undermining the 'credibility and reputation' of the station and fired her.

'I felt like I disappointed myself,' she said. 'I felt like I disappointed God.'

My evil boss

In 1993, Joe Gordon started a blog called the *Woolamalo Gazette*. The following year, he got a job at the book store Waterstones. He continued writing his blog and often used it to give glowing reviews of books he had enjoyed reading and to wax lyrical of the benefits and joys of regular reading.

All of which was the sort of content that his employers would have approved of. However, he also went on to rant about his 'sandal-wearing' manager who he called 'Evil Boss'. He also gave other details of his working life at 'Bastardstones'.

When his employers learned of this, they were not amused. They immediately suspended Gordon and opened an investigation into the matter. He was then called before a disciplinary panel and sacked for gross misconduct.

Gordon's case enraged many. Other bloggers wrote to him and said they would boycott

Waterstones in protest at his sacking. The Retail Books Association also backed him. A spokesman said, 'We feel it was heavy-handed and they have overreacted. They shouldn't use a hammer to crack a nut.'

Newspapers pointed out that, five years prior to Gordon's sacking, Waterstones had run an advertising campaign about the importance of freedom of speech. The award-winning campaign's slogan was: 'Adolf Hitler, Pol Pot & Mao Tse-Tung were right about one thing. The Power of Books.'

I am not ashamed of anything I wrote

To be fired because of your blog is known as being 'dooced' among the online community. Gordon is believed to be the first person to be dooced in the UK, but the phenomenon had already occurred a few times in the USA. Most famously, Jessica Cutler was fired as an aide to a senator after it was discovered that she was publishing details of her sex life via her blog, *Washingtonienne*.

'Most of my living expenses are thankfully subsidised by a few generous older gentlemen.

I'm sure I am not the only one who makes money on the side this way: how can anybody live on $25,000 a year?' She claimed specifically to have been sleeping with a high-level Republican who, she claimed, paid her $400 for sex.

After her sacking, Cutler gave an interview to a fellow blogger. She said, 'I am not ashamed of anything I wrote in the blog. And people are sad if they're interested in such a low-level sex scandal... I just think it's so silly. The blog is really about a bunch of nobodies... I still can't believe people care.'

However, people *did* care, so she made the best of her fame by posing nude for *Playboy* and writing a novel about her experiences. There have been reports that a television company is making a drama about her story. In 2006, *Giant* magazine named her one of eight rising stars of media and politics.

The Queen of the Sky

Ellen Simonetti was a hostess for the American airline Delta. She started a blog called 'The Queen Of The Sky' in which she recounted her adventures. Although the 29-year-old Texan kept herself and her airline anonymous in the blog, she blew her cover when she posted on it photographs of herself posing onboard a Delta aircraft. Unfortunately, in some of the images, her posture was slightly risqué. Delta immediately suspended her and she ultimately lost her job.

Clearly I haven't got the webcam angle quite right

In 2006, blog star La Petite Anglaise – real name Catherine – was sacked from the British accountancy firm where she had been employed as a secretary. Her blog was attracting over 3,000 daily readers but, once her bosses joined that number, her days at the firm were numbered.

Her superiors took offence at a number of her posts, including one that described how she accidentally flashed her breasts on camera while at work. She was fired and escorted from the building.

'Clearly I haven't got the webcam angle quite right and there I am, in my full glory, my v-necked jumper revealing a little more than I would have liked. I have managed not only to show my breasts but also to swear in front of Old School Boss. A sea of smirking faces swim into view. It would appear that their meeting room was already occupied too, with a full complement of London board members.'

I'd love a good long f***

Chris Bryant had been a vicar and head of the BBC's European Affairs before becoming MP for the solidly Labour constituency of Rhondda in South Wales. So imagine the shock of his constituents when, in November 2003, newspapers published photographs of Bryant wearing just his underpants, taken from an online gay dating website. On Bryant's Gaydar profile – under the username of Alfa101 – he described himself as a 'fit bloke' who is 'bright, solvent and single'.

The *Mail On Sunday*, which broke the story, also published messages he had sent to gay men via Gaydar. 'I'd love a good long f***,' read one. Another said, 'Horny bastard u interested in playing around?' Another: 'Oi mate so you want to come and f*** around.'

The press, naturally, had a field day with the

story, dubbing Bryant the 'Pants MP in a valley of shame'. Another photoshopped Bryant's face on to the body of Daffyd from *Little Britain* and added a speech bubble saying, 'No, I'm not the only gay in the valleys.'

After initially refusing to comment, Bryant apologised, saying, 'I'm sorry this has happened. I've always been open and honest about my private life but never sought to make an issue of it. I'm saddened that others have sought to do so.

'The important thing is the work that I do for my constituents as an MP. I will not myself be distracted from standing up for the people of the Rhondda.'

Standing up! Arf, arf! Bryant was allowed to keep his job and his constituents backed him with a solid 68 per cent of the vote at the 2005 general election.

She came in the night

Paul Marsden MP first hit the headlines in 2001 when he defected from Labour to the Liberal Democrats, claiming he was being bullied by Labour whips, whom he accused of being 'lousy and arrogant'. In 2005, he was back in the headlines when he moved back to Labour. It isn't just in politics, though, that the MP for Shrewsbury and Atcham is changeable.

In 2003, Marsden published poems about his colourful love-life on the internet. The married, libidinous Liberal Democrat was forced to admit to having had affairs after newspapers published the poems.

One poem read:

She came in the night,
She came in the night,
Dark hair, alive billowing as a
*   trapped kite*
Marching forward, confident and right,
Her hips swaying and her red lips tight
Then that smile so devastating in
*   its might,*
Tongue rippling across teeth so white.
Breasts rising as I feel the urge to bite.
Eyes stalking its prey, she's relishing
*   the fight.*
Who would mess with this amazing sight?
In awe of womanhood so sexual
*   and bright,*

☻ GREAT EMAIL DISASTERS ☻

A wondrous sweet smell exacerbates
  my plight,
Arching her back, stretched to its
  full height,
I am captured forever, dazzled by feminine
  light.
As she came in the night.

Lousy and arrogant, indeed!

CHAPTER TEN

THE SPOKEN WORD

Before we go, we cannot but salute modern technology for allowing us to capture the spoken word and enjoy its full potential for disaster. The pen may be mightier than the sword but the telephone can sometimes trump it.

In 1989, a telephone conversation between Prince Charles and Camilla Parker Bowles was intercepted and recorded by someone with a scanning device. However many times you read what Prince Charles said in this conversation, it never ceases to amaze.

Camilla was revealed to take a rather romantic line during the chat. 'I'd suffer anything for you,' she sighed, 'because that's love.' How sweet!

Prince Charles took a rather less charming line, telling his mistress that he'd 'like to live inside your trousers ... as a tampon.' What a charmer! Make a girl feel special, why don't you, Charlie? Sir Peter and his pink-nipple letters suddenly seem the pinnacle of romance and dignity in contrast to Charlie's sanitary soliloquy.

The very same year that Charles and Camilla were taped talking about toilet towels, Princess Diana also had a telephone conversation recorded. The conversation with her friend James Gilbey featured him regularly calling her 'squidgy' and telling her he loved her. She told Gilbey that future king and tampon-wannabe Prince Charles 'makes my life torture'. Both of these conversations were splashed across the papers, leaving the Windsors thoroughly red-faced.

In November 1990, Maggie Thatcher's Northern Ireland Under-Secretary Richard Needham was also embarrassed when phone calls of his were made public. His car-phone conversations were being recorded by terrorists and the details were leaked to the media. This was frightening enough in itself, but it became truly terrifying when he discovered that in one of the bugged chats to his wife he had described Thatcher as 'that silly cow'. He grovelled to the Prime Minister and kept his job.

Celtic FC chairman Brian Quinn too had reason to rue the telephone when he accidentally left a voicemail message on a teenager's phone. Thinking he was speaking to a PR officer, Quinn made a withering remark about 'the storm created by our esteemed manager'. The call followed a clash that Quinn had with the aforementioned manager, Martin O'Neill. However, he had misdialled and accidentally left the message on the phone of teenager Kayley Elkington.

This all occurred during the build-up to a clash with bitter local rivals Rangers, so the media naturally went to town on the affair. Quinn and O'Neill issued a joint statement denying there was a problem between them but the media were having none of this and pundits queued up to suggest that this was the end for O'Neill. As for Quinn, he quipped, 'When you reach my age, it is perhaps advisable to steer clear of newfangled devices like mobile phones.'

Some people, no matter what age they are, should also steer clear of television cameras. In 2004, during an ITV advertisement break, viewers in the Anglia TV region were treated to a weather forecast with a difference. Forecaster Sara Thornton got herself in a muddle during the report and suddenly blurted out 'fuck' and 'bugger'. To add irony to the incident, the report was broadcast during a break in the programme *All New TV's Naughtiest Blunders*.

Naturally, people with empty lives across the region phoned the station to complain. 'I was just dozing off on the sofa when suddenly I'm awoken by a torrent of swear words,' whined one viewer.

The moral of the story is: never doze off in front of the television or radio, because you don't know how many broadcasting cock-ups you might miss!

In 1984, President Ronald Reagan was preparing for his weekly radio address. Not realising that his microphone was switched on, the President told the nation: 'My fellow Americans, I am pleased to tell you that I just signed legislation that would outlaw Russia for ever. We begin bombing in five minutes.' Reagan has also been caught on microphone describing Polish leaders as a 'bunch of no-good, lousy bums' and admitting that his own economy was in 'a hell of a mess'.

Two decades on, George W Bush also found himself mucking up over a microphone when he was overheard at a press conference saying to Dick Cheney, 'There's Adam Clymer, major-league asshole from *The New York Times*.' Then there was that fantastic conversation he had with Tony Blair, when Bush said he wanted Hezbollah to 'stop doing this shit', not realising a microphone was picking up every word.

But Bush has perhaps been outdone in the calling-a-spade-a-spade stakes by Spanish politician Jose Bono. Talking privately to colleagues at a meeting, the President of Castilla La Mancha called Tony Blair *'un gilipollas integral'* which translates to English as a 'a complete dickhead'.

Speaking of dickheads, after politician and Chelsea FC supporter David Mellor left office because of his sex scandals, he became a football pundit, hosting Radio Five Live's weekly 606 supporters' phone-in programme. Here Mellor was forced to listen to some truly tiresome rants from frustrated football fanatics. As he handed over to the news after a particularly snoresome call, he was heard telling a colleague, 'Dull, wasn't it? I couldn't get that bloody fool off the line.'

In 1993, Mellor's former boss John Major had just finished being interviewed by the ITN political editor Michael Brunson. Believing the microphones had been turned off, the Prime Minister let fly at three of his cabinet colleagues. He called them 'bastards' and vowed to 'crucify them'. He then said, 'I want to understand, Michael, how such a complete wimp like me keeps winning everything.'

Didn't we all! The Conservatives were being plagued by a series of sex scandals at this point but Major protested, 'Even as an ex-Whip, I can't stop people sleeping with other people if they ought not.' And he should know...

The royals can be just as careless while miked-up. While skiing in Klosters, Prince Charles and his sons William and Harry were preparing for a press conference on the slopes. Not realising their microphones were switched on, the princes were heard having the following conversation.

Charles: *Do I put my arms around you?*

William: *No, don't, don't! You can take the horrible glasses away, too.*

Photographer: *Look as if you know each other, come on!*

Charles: *What do we do?*

William: *Keep smiling, keep smiling!*

Charles: *These people!*

Harry: *Someone's got a question.*

Charles: *Bloody people, I can't bear that man [the BBC's Nicholas Witchell]. I mean, he is so awful, he really is.*

A man who really was awful when he cocked up live on air was football manager turned pundit Ron Atkinson. Following a Champions League defeat for Chelsea in April 2004, broadcast live on ITV, Big Ron carried on discussing the game even after the broadcast finished. He began to discuss the Chelsea defender Marcel Desailly and said, 'He is what is known in some schools as a fucking thick lazy nigger.'

However, although the broadcast had finished in England, the discussion was still being broadcast in the Middle East. He was immediately dubbed 'Racist Ron' by the press and had to give up writing a column for the *Guardian* by mutual consent. He also resigned from his ITV commentary job. Since then, Atkinson has been forced to start the slow and humbling journey back up the broadcasting ladder.

The final word on microphone cock-ups goes to Southampton councillor Steve Broomfield, who had to apologise on radio and resign a committee position when he accidentally broadcast his thoughts on a kids' motorcycle display team over the loudspeakers at a fete. 'Oh no, they're not doing this again – get them off,' he snapped. 'They're boring. They're crap.' And on that wonderfully entertaining faux pas we'll sign off, though not before comforting ourselves that there will undoubtedly be more where that came from.

AFTERWORD

The 12-Step Plan To Avoiding Your Own Great Email Disaster

Having read the horror stories contained in this book, you are probably keener than ever to not become an unwitting celebrity of the worldwide web. Here are some tips to avoid an email disaster of your own. Follow these, and your chances of internet infamy will be much reduced.

1. When you receive an email containing a saucy joke and you think about forwarding

it around all your colleagues at work, don't do it. Just don't.

2. Some mail clients allow you to set your system to hold emails in the outbox for five minutes after you click the 'send' button. This allows you to cool off before final despatch and to check the email has been addressed to the correct person.

3. Do not email while drunk. Drink-driving ruins lives and so does drink-emailing.

4. Do not fill in any recipient in the 'To' field of the email until you have finished writing and checking the message.

5. Just as you wouldn't go on to prime-time television and blurt out all your secrets about your personal life, don't put any such secrets into an email.

6. Do not email while drunk.

7. Disable the 'reply all' option from your

email program. Yes, this may occasionally cause some small inconvenience when you do want to reply to everybody, but it will save you the huge inconvenience that can arise when you don't want to reply to all but accidentally do.

8. If you really must include something sensitive in an email then consider encrypting it. This means you obscure the information to anyone but the intended recipient. Ask a geek.

9. Seriously, don't email while drunk

10. Open a webmail account and do all your personal chatting there. Your company can easily snoop on your work email account, so, if you must send emails saying, 'My boss is a boring old tosser' or 'I had spectacular bum sex last night', it is far safer to send them via a Hotmail or Yahoo account.

11. Keep your password secret. That will prevent a suspicious husband or wife from

snooping through your messages and discovering you have been unfaithful. It will also prevent them sending out an email under your name claiming that you have a small penis. This is embarrassing enough if you are a man, but if you are a woman it must be peculiarly distressing.

12. Don't email while drunk.

If you have a great email disaster or other communications mishap you wish to share, please email greatemaildisasters@gmail.com You can remain anonymous if you prefer.